I0192192

Daughters
of the
Russian
Revolution

The right of Simon Webb to be identified
as the Author of the Work has been asserted by
him in accordance with the Copyright, Designs
and Patents Act 1988.

All rights reserved.

Published by The Langley Press, 2024

Daughters
of the
Russian
Revolution
Vera Zasulich
Alexandra Kollontai
Louise Bryant

Simon Webb

Also from the Langley Press

Karl Marx in London

The Life and Times of Ignatius Sancho:
An African in Eighteenth-Century London

John Lilburne: Gentleman, Leveller, Quaker

Joe Hill: Life and Death of an American Rebel

In Search of Leon Trotsky

For more from the Langley Press, please visit our website at
www.langleypress.co.uk

Contents

Vera Zasulich   7

Alexandra Kollontai   37

Louise Bryant   67

Revolutionary Women   98

Bibliography   103

Vera Zasulich

On the morning of the twenty-fourth of January 1878 a twenty-nine year-old woman named Vera Zasulich queued up to see Fyodor Trepov, the governor of Petersburg, then the capital of the Russian empire. Nearing seventy, Trepov had a fine long nose, and made up for the lack of hair on his head by sporting extensive whiskers above a clean-shaven chin. He was photographed in 1865 in a magnificent uniform with immaculate epaulettes and enough medals, badges and buttons to offer some protection against the bullets of a would-be assassin.

Like many Russian officials at the time, Trepov ran what we might call a regular 'surgery' at his home on Nevsky Prospect, perhaps the grandest of Petersburg's streets, and home to the famous Alexander Nevsky Monastery. People could bring him their problems and requests, rather like the *clientes* of ancient Roman noblemen, or petitioners to a medieval court. That morning, Vera Zasulich turned up in a new and rather large grey cloak, with her petition neatly written out.

Depending on how things went, Vera knew she might actually have to petition Trepov, so she had worked out an alternative name for herself, and was prepared to ask for a sort of reference or 'certificate of conduct' such as would be needed by a woman setting out on a career as a governess. Zasulich planned to call herself Elizaveta Kozlova, and had even gone to the trouble of sewing the initials 'EK' into the seams of her clothes, to support her cover story.

Soon after Vera and the other petitioners were let into *chez* Trepov, Zasulich found herself facing the man himself, across the top of his desk. She drew a Birmingham-made British Bull Dog revolver from under her cloak and began to fire at the governor. When she was sure that she had hit him, she dropped the gun and stood ready to be grabbed by his guards. In fact nothing happened for a few silent, eternal seconds: everybody froze in shock, then a guard punched Vera in the face and, as she lay sprawling on the floor, began to kick her.

Fyodor Trepov

The police and a doctor were called, the other petitioners vanished and Vera was hustled into a nearby room. An Inspector Kabat appeared, pale, small and shaking with nerves. He asked the obvious question, 'Why did you shoot him?' Calm and self-possessed, Vera replied, 'For Bogoliubov.'

News of the attempted assassination (Trepov was not killed, but lived on until 1889) spread rapidly throughout the city and beyond.

Already sensational, the story became even more juicy when it became clear what Vera had meant when she had told Kabat that she had shot Trepov 'for Bogoliubov'. In a blurry archive film of a procession related to the coronation of the last tsar, Nicholas II, in 1896, a beefy, moustachioed man who looks like a general can be seen gesturing angrily at the crowd, pointing repeatedly at his own head. He is telling the *hoi polloi* to take off their hats in the presence of such grand people. This is what Arkhip Bogoliubov failed to do.

Arkhip was a student in his early twenties who had been arrested (probably mistakenly) in the aftermath of a demonstration in Petersburg in December 1876. He was sentenced to fifteen years hard labour, but things got even worse after his gaol in Petersburg was visited, in July 1877, by our friend Fyodor Trepov. Bogoliubov refused to take off his hat in the presence of the old general, who personally knocked it off his head. Three hours later, Arkhip was flogged with birch rods, on Trepov's orders.

To a Russian peasant of the time, this would have been familiar treatment, though most country people would have doffed their headgear almost instinctively and thus avoided such chastisement. For a member of the intelligentsia to be punished in this way was unusual, and it seems that the shock and pain drove the young student quite mad. He developed a persecution complex, was placed in a mental hospital in Kazan in Russia's north-west, then, in 1887, was released into the custody of his father. It is not known exactly when he died. Shortly after the flogging that had caused Bogoliubov to lose his mind, some of his old comrades started to organise an attack on Trepov in retaliation for his harsh treatment; but they were beaten to it by Vera Zasulich.

Ordering the flogging of Bogoliubov was not the only crime of which Trepov was guilty, from the point of view of the enemies of the autocratic Russian empire. In those days, military officers loyal to the tsar often found themselves at war not with foreigners but with the tsar's own discontented subjects. Parts of Poland were then under Russian control, but many Poles wanted independence. Trepov was involved in the suppression of two Polish revolts, in the 1830s and

1860s respectively, and later commanded a cavalry regiment of gendarmes in Kyiv. These were, in effect, mounted armed police, or soldiers trained to deal with problems at home, rather than to fight wars against Russia's enemies abroad, or on her borders. Trepov had, therefore, distinguished himself in the area of Russia's military readiness to fight her own people, people who found themselves chafing under the yoke of tsarist rule.

Revolver of the type used by Vera Zasulich

While Vera languished in police custody, General Trepov was looked after at home. As if to show how important he was as an official, he was visited there by the tsar himself, Alexander II, known as 'the Liberator' because it was he who had abolished serfdom throughout much of his empire in 1861. In many countries that still have monarchies, such as the United Kingdom, the political role of the monarch is severely limited. Democratically elected parliaments and their leaders are in control, and under the system called 'constitutional monarchy' the king or queen becomes, at least in theory, a mere figurehead or symbol. This was not the case in Russia in 1878. The tsar was an autocrat: he had ultimate control over legislation, the armed services and even the Russian Orthodox Church.

Despite his reputation as a reformer, Tsar Alexander II was frequently threatened with assassination attempts. In March 1881, he was blown up on a street in Petersburg by a bomb thrown by Ignacy Hryniewiecki, a member of the Narodnaya Volya or 'People's Will' left-wing terrorist group, which had been founded the year after Vera Zasulich fired on General Trepov. Both the tsar and Hryniewiecki died shortly after the blast. Alexander made his final exit in the very room in the Winter Palace where he had signed the edict that freed the serfs, almost exactly twenty years earlier.

Six years later, a group of Petersburg students planned to mark the anniversary of the old tsar's assassination by killing his successor, Tsar Alexander III. Like Ignacy Hryniewiecki, they were also members of Narodnaya Volya. On the first of March 1887 three of them were arrested on Nevsky Prospect, the Petersburg street where Vera Zasulich had shot Trepov. The trio were carrying bombs, and the police rounded up several more members of the group. Among those who were later hanged was Alexander Ulyanov, the elder brother of Vladimir Ulyanov, known to history as Vladimir Lenin. Despite the efforts of people like Ulyanov, the third Tsar Alexander managed to escape assassination: he died of kidney disease in Crimea in 1894.

Despite her comparative youth, Vera Zasulich's stint in prison in 1878 was not her first taste of such confinement. She had spent the years 1869-73 locked up because of her association with the slightly older Russian revolutionary Sergei Nechaev. In the year Vera's first imprisonment began, Nechaev fled abroad, where he kept company with such ex-pat compatriots as the anarchist Michael Bakunin. Bakunin was enchanted by Nechaev, whom he called 'my boy'. In 1872, however, Bakunin's young friend was extradited from Switzerland back to Russia, where he died in prison ten years later, at the age of just thirty-five, from a deadly combination of dropsy and scurvy.

11

Sergei Nechaev

The direct cause of Vera Zasulich's first imprisonment was a coded letter sent to her from abroad by Nechaev. The authorities easily decoded the letter: it seems that Sergei had not intended it to be too hard for them. At the same time, he had sent revolutionary leaflets to nearly four hundred other Russians, hoping that these would incriminate them, cause them to be arrested and imprisoned, and therefore become radicals. This brutal scheme was the political equivalent of deliberately sending a batch of illegal child pornography to an acquaintance, hoping that he will end up in prison.

The parcel project was based on Nechaev's habit of collecting the addresses of everyone he met. It was a more elaborate version of an earlier plan where he had collected the signatures of his followers. The signatures and addresses, carefully saved, put these people in Nechaev's power. Running out of addresses to which to send his compromising parcels, in 1869 Nechaev resorted to sending them out at random to people and institutions with which he had not previously had any contact.

The victims of Nechaev's parcel scheme were likely to be caught, as Vera Zasulich was, because many were under police surveillance already, and anything sent to them from abroad was likely to be intercepted and investigated. Some of the panicked recipients of the poisonous parcels turned them in to the police straight away, and no doubt some merely burned them and were never bothered by the authorities. Vera had less chance of escaping notice: many of the letters accompanying other people's parcels mentioned Vera. She was even more liable to arrest because the authorities had managed to connect her, through her sister Alexandra and her mother Ekaterina, to an associate of Nechaev's called Liudmilla Kolachevskaia.

Nechaev's unhesitating betrayal of his past contacts is reminiscent of the actions of the man posing as a scholar called Professor Coram in Conan Doyle's 1904 story *The Adventure of the Golden Pince-Nez*. Here Anna, 'Coram's' much younger wife, travels to a secluded cottage called Yoxley Old Place in Kent to confront the bogus professor with his crimes, and retrieve some documents which should prove the innocence of her young lover, currently languishing in a Siberian salt mine.

At first Vera Zasulich was imprisoned in Petersburg's notorious Lithuanian Castle, a gaol where nothing could feel at home except darkness, damp and mould. The filth and stench of the place were appalling, and Vera was kept there in solitary confinement, with no access to books or the means to communicate with anyone on the outside. After a few desperate months, she was transferred to Petersburg's Peter and Paul fortress, which the reforms of Tsar Alexander II had turned into a comparatively pleasant place. Years later, when Leon Trotsky was imprisoned here, he was able to turn his cell into a comfortable combination of a library, office and bedroom, and even enjoyed conjugal visits from his second wife, during one of which Leon and Natalia conceived one of their sons.

In Peter the Great's fortress on the Neva, Vera Zasulich was able to occupy her time by reading voraciously, enjoying access to a wide range of literature, some of which was shockingly radical in the imperial Russian context. Zasulich had a tendency to escape into books, which was noticed by friends and acquaintances later, in very different settings.

Nechaev's reckless use (or abuse) of people was entirely consistent with his *Catechism of a Revolutionary*, written in the same year he sent out his compromising parcels and letters. This chilling document, to which Bakunin may have contributed, insisted that revolutionaries should be a hard, ruthless, inhuman creatures, who judged other people only in terms of their usefulness or otherwise to the revolutionary cause.

In the *Catechism*, women are said to fall into one of three categories, each with their uses. 'Frivolous, thoughtless, and vapid women' should be blackmailed and otherwise compromised so that they become 'transformed' into unwilling 'slaves'. Female revolutionaries who have 'not yet achieved a passionless and austere revolutionary understanding' must be 'driven on to make compromising declarations' to the point where some of them will be 'destroyed' but others turned into 'genuine revolutionaries'. The *Catechism*'s third and last category of women are those who are already 'genuine revolutionaries' and are 'the most valuable of our treasures'. Further proof, if proof were needed, that a woman should be very suspicious if a man starts referring to her as a 'treasure'.

The *Catechism* makes it clear that Nechaev did not only plan to destroy some members of his second category of women, the female rebels who were not (yet) entirely committed to the cause, in which group, it seems, he had mentally placed Vera Zasulich. In one English translation of the *Catechism*, words like 'destroy', 'destruction' and 'destructive' occur sixteen times, though the whole thing comes to fewer than two thousand words. At times it looks as if Sergei wants to destroy everything, including 'the social order and the civilized world with all its laws, moralities, and customs, and with all its generally accepted conventions', in short 'the whole filthy order'.

If his *Catechism of a Revolutionary* truly reflected his views, then it is not surprising that the tsar, whose Winter Palace Nechaev wanted some of his followers to 'penetrate', took special care to see that Sergei stayed behind bars, once he was back in Russia. The original plan had been to exile him to Siberia for twenty years (until he would have been forty-five) but his imperial highness insisted that Nechaev spend the rest of his life in prison, in cell number one of the Alexis Ravelin of the Peter and Paul Fortress in Petersburg. The tsar also made sure he received weekly reports on Sergei's progress in this place.

Among the well-known prisoners kept in Peter the Great's Petersburg fortress were the anarchist Peter Kropotkin, who managed to escape in 1876, when Nechaev had already been there for four years. Other famous prisoners included the writers Fyodor Dostoevsky and Maxim Gorky, the future Yugoslavian leader Josip Tito, the Bolshevik Leon Trotsky, the aforementioned Alexander Ulyanov, Lenin's older brother, and the author Nikolay Chernyshevsky, of whom more later. Vetrova, a student from a later generation, deliberately burned herself to death while imprisoned in the fortress in 1897. In his autobiography *My Life*, Trotsky claimed that he had started his own 'revolutionary work to the accompaniment of the Vetrova demonstrations'. These were widespread student protests: although the details of Vetrova's death are blurry, one version is that she poured lamp-oil over herself, then set light to it.

Sergei and Vera had both been caught up in revolutionary circles in Petersburg, a city to which Vera had come in search of work in 1866, at the age of seventeen. In Peter the Great's city on the Neva she had worked as a clerk, but in the evenings she would tutor workers and attend such underground events as Nechaev's candle-lit readings of revolutionary writings. In the hushed atmosphere of these clandestine gatherings, pictures of the French revolutionaries Maximilien Robespierre and Louis Saint-Just would be displayed to the assembled company.

In the Russian context, Nechaev's candle-lit readings sound a little like intimate prayer-meetings in the Orthodox Christian tradition, complete with the ikons that are so characteristic of the Russian Church. In *Angel of Vengeance*, her 2009 book about Vera Zasulich, Ana Siljak traces her heroine's devotion to the people's struggle back to a youthful religious devotion.

In his autobiography, Trotsky asserted that he had not had a 'black' childhood like many of his Russian contemporaries, who grew up homeless and hungry. Neither did he have a bright, happy childhood, as his parents had rather neglected him and his siblings. Instead he had had a 'grey' childhood; and the same might be said of Vera Zasulich, who was Trotsky's senior by thirty years.

Unlike Trotsky, the son of a prosperous Jewish farmer in Ukraine, Vera Zasulich came of a noble Polish family, but from a branch that had hit hard times. She was born in the summer of 1849 in the Russian town of Gzhatsk, over a hundred miles west of Moscow. To show how the lives of revolutionaries interlock, 1849 was the year that a thirty-one year-old German called Karl Marx settled in London, where he would live for the rest of his life. Zasulich's home town of Gzhatsk was re-named Gagarin in 1968, after the death of Yuri Gagarin, the Russian cosmonaut who had become the first man in space, in 1961. Gagarin himself had been born in 1934 at Klushino, a few miles to the north.

Though born at Gzhatsk, Vera was not to live there for very long. Her father, a retired army captain and also an alcoholic, died in 1853 when she was only three years old. Now an impoverished widow with four children and another on the way, Vera's mother Feoktista Zasulich sent her away to Biaklovo, to live on the estate of some wealthy cousins. Vera therefore became that fascinating creature, the poor relation in a grand household, rather like Fanny Price in Jane Austen's 1814 novel *Mansfield Park*. Fanny's chance to escape from her rather downtrodden position is to accept a proposal of marriage from her cousin Edmund, at the age of eighteen. Vera Zasulich was cut from a different cloth. She sought gainful employment in Petersburg, at the age of seventeen, having only just graduated from high school.

Not that Vera was not offered romantic opportunities. That Nechaev had added Vera to his list of people he wanted to go to prison for the cause may not be entirely unconnected to the fact that his comrade, who had been close to him in Petersburg, had refused to go into exile with him, even though he declared that he was in love with her. Presumably, their time on the lam would have been even more scandalous and unconventional, to some minds, than the elopement of Maria with Henry Crawford in *Mansfield Park*, or Lydia Bennet's disappearance with the disreputable George Wickham in *Pride and Prejudice*.

While we might be tempted to compare Vera's position as the poor relation living with a grand family to various set-ups described by Jane Austen and other English novelists, Ana Siljak reminds us that the novel that would have been very much on Vera's mind was Nikolay Chernyshevsky's *What Is to be Done?* which was published in 1863. This should not be confused with Lenin's celebrated 1902 pamphlet that has the same title. That Lenin chose to re-use Chernyshevsky's title shows the continuing influence of the novel nearly fifty years after its original publication.

If *What Is to be Done?* inspired thinkers like Lenin, born over forty years after the novel's author, the effect of the book on the discontented Russian youth of the eighteen-sixties and seventies is easy to imagine, though as Siljak points out, as a novel it leaves much to be desired. Like

Vera Pavlovna, the heroine of Chernyshevsky's book, Vera Zasulich struck out for independence, lived in an unconventional way and even tried to set up a workers' cooperative with one of her sisters. Unfortunately the Zasulich sisters' commune of seamstresses did not enjoy lasting success.

A 'marker' shared by Russian rebels who acted on the ideas in Chernyshevsky's book was that they tended to live collectively, in shared houses or apartment-blocks, like some modern students for whom there is no space in their college's campus accommodation, or who prefer not to live in halls of residence at all. For nineteenth-century Russians of the older generation, or younger people who followed the moral teachings of the Orthodox Church, such arrangements must have seemed scandalous, especially when single women were living unchaperoned in close proximity to men. As in houses shared by various types of radical students today, some of the mini-communes formed by devotees of Chernyshevsky were consciously experimenting with new ways of living, and showing a bold disregard for the domestic conventions and routines that are still a preoccupation, if not an unhealthy obsession, for many right down to our own time.

What Is to be Done? was Chernyshevsky's response to an earlier and far superior novel by one of Russia's most abiding literary figures, Ivan Turgenev. *Fathers and Sons* (1862) includes a character called Bazarov, a young nihilist who cannot have been based on Nechaev, who was practically unknown when *Fathers and Sons* was published. Turgenev's novel depicts Bazarov as coarse, offensive, disruptive, disconcerting and ultimately clueless, but the Russian nihilists of the upcoming generation embraced 'Bazarovism' and modelled themselves in part on this fictional misfit. Although Turgenev's Bazarov cannot have been based on Nechaev, Dostoevsky's 1872 novel *The Demons* was inspired by the author's concern about the influence of people like Vera's dangerous friend.

Turgenev's *Fathers and Sons* is a kind of thought-experiment in the form of a novel. What would happen, the author might have asked himself, if we introduce one of these new nihilist young people into a typical Russian country house, owned by a likeable minor aristocrat? Part of the interest of the book lies in the fact that it sets out for us a typical or indicative Russian country set-up. In fact, as if to enhance the effectiveness of his book as a mirror of Russian country life, Turgenev hawks his Bazarov around, putting him into various social settings, including the urban home of an eccentric female libertine, his own parents' modest estate, the very well-run establishment of an attractive young widow, and the country home of his student friend Arkady, whose father is the likeable minor aristocrat mentioned above.

There is much to be admired and much to take exception to in all of the places Bazarov visits. His own father, an otherwise lovable retired army doctor, beats his servants on occasion, and Arkady's father, Nikolai Kirsanov, cannot seem to decide whether the employees on his estate are fools or rogues. The Kirsanov estate, Marino, is badly-run on antiquated lines, and Nikolai relies on regular subsidies from his brother Pavel to keep the old place afloat. Nikolai, a widower, has taken his dead housekeeper's beautiful young daughter as a mistress, and has fathered an illegitimate child with her.

Although the reader might see ways that the lives of these people could be improved, for instance by a concerted effort to improve communication between the representatives of the different social classes, Bazarov's attitude – the rejection of everything – seems unhelpful to say the least. While Bazarov professes to believe in absolutely nothing, some of the later nihilists took this to the extreme of wanting to *destroy* everything. If nothing else, Turgenev's *Fathers and Sons* introduced its first readers to the ideas, or, at least, the attitudes of the nihilists of the time. It gave many a point of reference to relate to later shocking manifestations of nihilist ideas.

It may seem strange that mere novels had such a huge influence on Russian politics at the time, but the reader must remember that Vera Zasulich lived in the days when many of Russia's greatest authors were alive and writing. Leo Tolstoy, who died in 1910, was enormously influential, as were Fyodor Dostoevsky, and the playwright and story-writer Anton Chekhov.

These authors and others addressed the political situation in Russia, often showing up the pointlessness of the lives of the aristocrats, the pettiness of the bourgeoisie, and the hopeless poverty of the peasants. Turgenev's *Sketches From a Hunter's Album*, a series of short stories published ten years before his *Fathers and Sons*, presents a series of pen-pictures of peasants living in desperate conditions, oppressed by their cruel and often stupid landlords and local officials. While many of Russia's greatest writers embraced politics and depicted social conditions in their fiction, political figures such as the theorist Alexander Herzen, the Bolshevik politician Alexandra Kollontai (of whom more later) and even Vera Zasulich tried their hands at fiction, to put their ideas into a more digestible form.

Readers familiar with the history of German literature may recall how practically a whole generation of depressed young German men modelled themselves on the eponymous hero of Goethe's novel *Sorrows of Young Werther*, published in 1774. Like Werther, they wore yellow waistcoats, and some even went so far as to commit suicide, as Werther does near the end of the novel. Beyond Werther, Turgenev's Bazarov and the nihilists of *What Is to be Done?* it is hard to think of more works of literature on whom people have based their lives, even changing their dress-code, behaviour and vocabulary. Perhaps the most striking twentieth-century example would be Jack Kerouac's cult novel *On the Road* (1957) which still inspires young and old to pile into rickety cars and vans and go on long vaguely-planned journeys.

Despite the time in prison that followed her refusal to run off with Nechaev, Vera may have dodged a bullet, so to speak, by refusing to go abroad with the slim, handsome, intense-looking revolutionary. He was a dangerous, unstable character: the immediate reason for his decision to flee Russia in 1869 was his involvement in the murder of a student called Ivan Ivanov, who had expressed doubts about Nechaev's ideas and his approach to leadership, in October of that year. Sergei and some comrades had beaten, strangled and shot Ivanov, then hid his body under the ice of a lake in Moscow's Petrovsky Park. Among the murderers who ambushed Ivanov that November night were Vera Zasulich's brother-in-law, Peter Uspensky.

Though Uspensky was supposed to be a comrade-in-arms, and had acted as his accomplice in a murder, it seems that Nechaev did not hesitate to ask his wife, Vera's sister Alexandra, to flee abroad with him, in the same way he asked Vera herself. Alexandra also refused, because she was nine months pregnant. Nechaev had to make do with his third choice, an older married woman called Varvara Alexandrovskaya.

Nechaev and his accomplices had made a poor job of concealing Ivanov's body, and had even left some handy clues at the scene. While their leader fled abroad, the authorities were able to round up large numbers of Sergei's followers, and a prosecutor called Phillip Chemadurov began to sift through the mountains of files relating to the case.

By March of 1871 Chemadurov felt that he had mastered enough of the facts to be able to say that there was not sufficient evidence to continue to detain Vera Zasulich, and that she should be released. She was, however, re-arrested after only ten days, and sent not to prison but into exile, to a small town called Kresty in Russia's Novgorod province, about a hundred miles to the south-east of Petersburg. Just a few weeks later, Vera was allowed to return home.

Although he believed her to be innocent, Chemadurov the prosecutor hoped that, as a one-time member of Nechaev's circle, Vera would be able to testify against disciples whom Chemadurov believed *were* guilty. But when Vera mounted the witness stand in Petersburg in the June of 1871 she said as little as possible, contradicted her earlier statements, and aired her grievances about her treatment at the hands of the authorities. As would happen later, when Vera was tried for the attempted assassination of Trepov, the trial of the Nechaevites turned into an indictment of the terrible political and social conditions in Russia. Various witnesses agreed that Nechaev himself was guilty as hell, but the Russian authorities had not yet been able to capture him.

As well as having a murder hanging over his head, Sergei Nechaev was a liar, almost, it would seem, on principle. He claimed to be from peasant stock, but in fact he was from a family of shopkeepers in the textile town of Ivanovo, over one hundred and fifty miles north-east of Moscow. While many believed him to be a university student, he was never formally registered as such, though much of his activism took place in student circles.

If Vera Zasulich had followed Nechaev into exile, the pair may not have married. Followers of the new way of life described in Chernyshevsky's *What Is to be Done?* often experimented with platonic relationships, or, at the other extreme, what we would now call open marriages. Vera Pavlovna, Chernyshevsky's heroine, ends up living in a *ménage à quatre* with her husband, her lover and her husband's lover.

Later Sergei Nechaev was involved in some very shady business involving Bakunin and a publisher to whom Bakunin was reluctantly bound by a contract. Nechaev wrote to the publisher, threatening to kill him if he did not tear up the contract. In 1872 Karl Marx produced Nechaev's letter at the Hague congress of the International Workingmen's Association, also known as the First International. The letter added justification to the IWA's decision to expel both Bakunin and Nechaev.

After she had testified at the trial of the Nechaevites, Vera went to live in the Russian city of Tver with her mother, her sister Ekaterina and Ekaterina's husband, Lev Nikiforov. Tver is about a hundred miles north-west of Moscow. Here Vera and her family came to the attention of the authorities again, this time by setting up a radical reading group based in the city's Orthodox seminary. As a result, Lev, Ekaterina and Vera found themselves in exile in the tiny town of Soligalich, over three hundred miles north-east of Moscow. Here once again Vera immersed herself in books, and found herself particularly inspired by the writings of the exiled Russian anarchist Michael Bakunin, a native of Tver province himself, and at one time a close associate of Nechaev.

Desperate to get out of Soligalich and become involved in Bakunin-inspired radical action, Vera got permission to transfer to the city of Kharkiv in Ukraine. There she made contact with a group called the Southern Rebels, based in two apartments in Kyiv, nearly three hundred miles to the west. As we shall see when we come to meet Zasulich's slightly older contemporary Katherine Breshkovsky, at the time radical Russia was still smarting from the embarrassment of the 'to the people' movement, when would-be revolutionaries had disguised themselves as peasants and tried to preach socialism in the villages. Inspired by Bakunin, and recent rebellions in the Balkans, the Southern Rebels went to the people as the Narodniks had done, but this time with weapons and plans for an armed revolution.

The peasants who were supposed to rise up and follow the likes of Vera Zasulich into battle against the tsar and his armies soon detected that the thinly-disguised intellectuals who insisted on lecturing them had only the vaguest idea of how a revolution could be brought about, or what would follow it. At last, Vera was advised by her friend Lev Deich, who later became her lover, to go to the city of Elizavetgrad (now Kropyvnytskyi in Ukraine) where the rebels had moved their headquarters.

As the rebels' organisation disintegrated, Deich persuaded Vera to move again, this time to Penza in Russia's north-easterly Volga region, where her sister Ekaterina and her husband owned an estate. It was at Penza that Vera read about the flogging of Arkhip Bogoliubov in prison in Petersburg. She returned to the Russian capital, determined to kill the man who had ordered Bogoliubov's punishment, General Fyodor Trepov.

When Vera Zasulich was tried for the attempted murder of Trepov, her past experience with the Russian justice system must surely have persuaded her that she was now destined to a second and even longer stint behind bars. She was in for a surprise. The presiding judge was the distinguished Anatoly Koni, an enlightened liberal who was very much in favour of reform, and even wrote poetry. At thirty-four, he was young for a judge, being a member of Zasulich's own generation. Koni's 1898 portrait by Ilya Repin, one of Russia's greatest artists, shows a sad, harassed man who nevertheless looks both tough and compassionate.

The court-room Vera faced was similar to the kind she would have encountered in England and the United States at this time. Thanks to the efforts of the reforming Tsar Alexander II, Russia now had jury trials for such cases, and the accused were defended by professional counsel. Juries could even go beyond deciding if a prisoner was guilty or innocent, and give an opinion about sentencing. In theory, a jury could even decide if prisoners should not receive any punishment for crimes they were found to have committed.

In Vera's case, the jury found the would-be assassin of General Trepov not guilty, despite the fact that there were plenty of witnesses, and the man still bore the scars from her attack. What had happened was that Zasulich's defence lawyer had turned the tables on the court and set out the abuses of which Trepov was guilty, so that at some point it felt as if Trepov himself were on trial, not Vera at all. In this scenario, the gunwoman became the innocent party, a conscientious vigilante, a righter of wrongs.

That Vera herself remained remarkably calm and level-headed all through the proceedings just added to the jury's impression that here was a rational woman who was merely fighting for justice. The fact that she looked rather young for her age might also have helped her cause: she was bony and angular, like a girl of fourteen. Although she had donned a smart new cloak before her encounter with Trepov, Vera later became well-known for the shabby (often black) clothes and big, rough boots she wore. She also cut her hair short, in the style of many female Russian radicals of the time, and smoked endless cigarettes.

If she had managed to kill or maim Trepov things might have gone differently, but the jury's sensational verdict of not guilty meant that she could walk out of the court-room straight away. Attempts by the authorities to re-arrest her were foiled by the crowds, who fought off officials and protected their new heroine. After a time living in hiding in Petersburg, Zasulich fled to Switzerland.

Vera's case was sufficiently widely-known and discussed to have come to the attention of the Irish author Oscar Wilde (1854-1900). Wilde's first play, *Vera; or, The Nihilists* was loosely based on Zasulich's attempt to kill Trepov, though it is set many years earlier and centres on an attempt by a fictional nihilist called Vera Sabouroff to kill the tsar. Though most of the action is supposed to happen in 1800, the characters in Wilde's play talk about the recent liberation of the serfs (which happened much later, in 1861) and about trains and telegrams.

These clumsy mistakes are just some of the aspects that make Wilde's play a little ridiculous. Other factors include its melodramatic plot and its use of rather stilted English. One character, Prince Paul Maraloffski, comes over as an unexpected refugee from one of Wilde's later comedies. The prince, who is prime minister of Russia, is forever making witty, paradoxical remarks, and spouting humorous observations, such as 'experience, the name men give to their mistakes' and 'to make a good salad is a much more difficult thing than cooking accounts'. It is hard to see how any writer could have made Prince Paul's character fit in a tragic play about political assassination.

Wilde's Vera Sabouroff is from much humbler origins than Vera Zasulich: she is the daughter not of impoverished aristocrats but of an inn-keeper. She is driven into a desperate nihilist group in St Petersburg because she is looking for revenge: her brother has been imprisoned by the tsarist authorities. This resembles the story of Vladimir Lenin, who only became politically active after the execution of his brother Sasha, on political charges, in 1887, seven years after Wilde completed his play.

Chosen by lot to kill the new, young, reforming tsar after the old tsar has been shot dead, Vera discovers that the new man in the palace is none other than the nice young fellow who has been attending her nihilist group for some months, with whom she has inadvertently fallen in love. She finds a way out of this embarrassing pickle by stabbing herself with the knife she was supposed to use for the regicide. The trope of the prince in disguise is a reminder that Wilde also wrote fairy tales for children. There is a well-known Russian example: Pushkin's verse rendering of the tale of the tsar Saltan. Here Prince Gvidón turns into a mosquito, a fly and then a bumble-bee.

Although Wilde's play plays some wild variations on the theme of the young female assassin, some of the stories that were circulating about Vera Zasulich after her sensational acquittal were almost as melodramatic and unlikely. The *New York Times* reported as fact that Vera had been sexually assaulted by Trepov, that her sweetheart Bogoliubov had given him a sound beating, and that the imprisonment and flogging of Bogoliubov was simply Trepov's revenge. In a heaping of revenge on revenge worthy of a minor English renaissance tragedy, the *Times* asserted that Vera had tried to kill Trepov because he had ordered the beating of her lover.

Vera; or, The Nihilists is not a great play, any more than Chernyshevsky's *What Is to be Done?* is a great novel. It has not enjoyed anything like the influence exerted by Chernyshevsky's book, and has certainly not met with anything like the continued success of Wilde's later comedies, especially his theatrical masterpiece *The Importance of Being Earnest*, which premiered in 1895 and has seldom been off the stage since. In fact Wilde's serious plays have always had a bumpy time of it: the best-known, *Salomé* (1891) is too short to work as a conventional evening at the theatre, and too poetic for many English audiences. An attempt to stage *Salomé* in London in 1892 was stopped because of a ban on depicting biblical characters on stage.

An unofficial form of censorship also quashed the first London production of *Vera* in 1882: in that year, both Tsar Alexander II of Russia and the U.S. President James Garfield were assassinated, and there was a feeling that even showing a fictional tsar being killed onstage might be a little tactless. The Russian authorities are supposed to have intimated as much through diplomatic channels, and it was remembered that the Prince of Wales (later King Edward VII) was married to a sister of the new tsarina. Garfield had been killed using a British Bulldog revolver similar to the one Vera had used on General Trepov.

A New York production of Wilde's *Vera* closed after just a few days in August 1883, having received a mixed reception from the critics. The *New York Times* review stated that '[*Vera*] comes as near failure as an ingenious and able writer can bring it'. This was like one of those school reports which remark that the student 'could do better'.

As we know, a suicidal female nihilist also features in Arthur Conan Doyle's story *The Adventure of the Golden Pence-Nez*, which was first published in *The Strand Magazine* in 1904. Here, as often happens in Doyle's Sherlock Holmes stories, the great detective is investigating the tail-end of a melodramatic story that began overseas. Really, it is surprising how many of these hot-headed foreign adventurers ended up in London, or close to the English capital, in those days.

In *The Golden Pince-Nez*, Anna, the one-time nihilist who had inadvertently committed the murder that brings Holmes and Watson to Yoxley Old Place in Kent, is not the real villain of the piece. That is the apparently harmless Professor Coram, actually a nihilist who fled Russia with the party funds and betrayed his comrades.

By the time Oscar Wilde wrote *Vera* in 1880, the real Vera, Vera Zasulich, had been in exile for two years. She had begun her exile in Switzerland in the tiny village of Sion in the Rhône valley, with Dmitri Klements, a comrade with whom she had shared a tiny flat in Petersburg, while she was hiding from the authorities to avoid being re-arrested after her acquittal. The pair borrowed the chalet of a friend of Klements', and had a very Swiss time of it, hiking in the mountains, climbing rocks, sleeping in the open air or sheltering in shepherds' huts. The presence of the famous Vera Zasulich could not go unnoticed by her fellow exiled Russians in Switzerland, and she soon found herself being lionised by the cream of the Russian radicals.

While her fame was based on an attempted murder, and her story had led to a veritable craze for violent political action, Vera herself was turning against the idea of terrorism, and began to write in favour of more peaceful means of change.

Whereas she had previously been inspired by the ideas of Nechaev and Bakunin, who were anarchists, she now converted to Marxism, and co-founded the Emancipation of Labour group, the first Russian Marxist organisation. The other founders included some of the earliest Russians to embrace Marxist ideas; people like Georgi Plekhanov, Pavel Axelrod and Leo Deutsch.

By this time Marx himself was sixty-one, and had been living in London for thirty years. In 1879, the year Vera Zasulich had to become accustomed to life in exile, the father of Marxism enjoyed a memorable lunch at the exclusive Devonshire Club in London. This was hosted by an aristocratic politician with the improbable name of Sir Mountstuart Elphinstone Grant Duff, part of whose motivation in arranging the lunch was to meet the author of *Capital*, the first volume of which had been published twelve years earlier.

Grant Duff found the German to be interesting and not unpleasant company. Sounding him out on the situation in Russia, he listened as Marx predicted 'a great and not distant crash'. This, Marx prophesied, might lead to a revolution that would spread to his native Germany, 'taking there the form of a revolt against the existing military system'. 1879, the year of Marx's lunch with Grant Duff, was also the year the man who would become known as Leon Trotsky was born, in what is now Ukraine.

In 1880, the year after Marx's slap-up lunch at the Devonshire club, Vera Zasulich turned down the chance to become the editor of a magazine called *The Nihilist*, though the scheme had the approval of Marx himself, and may have attracted backing from Marx's wealthy friend, Frederick Engels. Siljak takes this as an indication of Vera's determination to abandon nihilism and embrace Marxism. But there was a problem. The Russian Marxists, avidly reading versions of the first volume of Marx's book *Capital*, were concerned that it might be impossible, strictly speaking, to apply Marxist theory to conditions in Russia. They had run up against an issue that would dog Russian Marxism for decades.

In *Capital* and elsewhere, Marx had prophesied that, with the advance of industrial capitalism, the bourgeoisie, the owners of the factories, would come to supplant the land-owning aristocracy as the masters of the earth. Eventually they would find themselves face-to-face with the far more numerous proletariat: the land-dwelling peasantry and their old masters, the aristocracy, would have withered away. Thanks to their superior numbers, Marx prophesied, the proletariat would inevitably gain control, and 'the dictatorship of the proletariat' would be established.

For Russians yearning for a Marxist revolution in their own country, the outlook was, therefore, bleak. Russia's economy was dominated by agriculture, the land-owning aristocracy were all-powerful, and the numbers of bourgeoisie and proletarians were surely far from the critical mass needed to herald the longed-for hegemony of the industrial workers. Would Russia have to wait, perhaps for decades or longer, for the conditions for the right kind of revolution to appear?

Vera wrote to Marx in London from Geneva in February 1881, asking him a question that she described as 'urgent' and 'a life-and-death question above all for our socialist party'. 'In one way or another,' she went on, 'even the personal fate of our revolutionary socialists depends upon your answer to the question'.

The question Vera asked was, could the traditional communes that existed among the Russian peasants be a basis for a worthwhile revolution, or would the Russian revolutionaries have to wait, perhaps for 'many centuries' until Russian capitalism reached 'something like the level of development attained in Western Europe?' Vera concluded her letter with a plea to Marx to send a detailed answer 'that you would allow us to translate and publish in Russia'.

Given Vera's celebrity, and the importance his correspondent and her comrades were likely to attach to his reply, it is hardly surprising that Marx, who was not a well man by this stage, went through several drafts before he finally arrived at a shortish text to send off to Geneva. Writing from his very respectable suburban terraced house at number forty-one, Maitland Park Road, London, Marx assured her that the theories and predictions in his book *Capital* were '*expressly* restricted to *the countries of Western Europe*'. Russia, he implied, was a law unto itself:

The analysis in *Capital* therefore provides no reasons either for or against the vitality of the Russian commune. But the special study I have made of it, including a search for original source-material, has convinced me that the commune is the fulcrum for social regeneration in Russia.

Despite this welcome *imprimatur* from the very father of Marxism, many continued to doubt that Russia could be the cradle of the right kind of revolution. One prominent revolutionary who persisted in his doubts on this score, even years after the revolution of 1917, was the Ukrainian Leon Trotsky. In some of his later writings, Trotsky tried to use the theory of Russia's status as a less-than-perfect setting for the rise of workers' power as an explanation for the failures of the revolution, and particularly for the disastrous rise of Stalin.

Trotsky first met Vera Zasulich in 1902 in London, when she would have been over fifty and he in his early twenties. He wrote a lot about her in various books and other writings, in part perhaps because she was so famous, but also because he seems to have found her interesting in herself.

Leon had escaped from enforced exile in Siberia, where he had left his first wife Alexandra and their two small daughters. He had come to the English capital in search of the people responsible for the radical *Iskra* Russian-language newspaper, which had moved to the city earlier that year. The *Iskra* comrades were the backbone of the Russian Social Democratic Labour Party, the direct ancestor of the Bolsheviks and the communist rulers of Russia after the revolution of 1917.

'*Iskra*' in Russian means 'The Spark'. The dominant personality of the *Iskra* group was Vladimir Lenin, but other Russian exiles including Vera Zasulich made their contributions. Even when he was writing from exile in Siberia, pieces by Trotsky had been published in *Iskra*, and it is no surprise that the group welcomed the tall, striking comrade. Lenin had hoped that he would find a new ally in the intense young Ukrainian, but the influence of others, including members of the 'old guard' like Vera Zasulich, drew several, including Trotsky, away from Lenin during these years.

In London, *Iskra* was published from the building now known as the Marx Memorial Library and Workers' School on Clerkenwell

Green, where the office where Lenin worked is preserved as a kind of room-sized time-capsule.

Leon Trotsky later gave his impressions of Vera in his autobiography *My Life,* in his own book on Lenin, and elsewhere. From him we learn that some members of the *Iskra* group were sharing a house, in the style of the radicals in Chernyshevsky's *What Is to be Done?* Trotsky was shown the way to this urban commune, which featured a 'common room' where the comrades 'drank coffee, smoked, and engaged in endless discussions'. 'This room,' the newcomer remembered, 'thanks chiefly to Zasulich, but not without help from [Julius] Martov, was always in a state of rank disorder'.

In London the Ukrainian saw rather more of Vera and Julius than he did of Lenin himself, as they shared a house. Trotsky came to admire Vera not just for her 'heroic past' but for her 'sharp mind', her wide reading and her 'psychological insight'. He found her 'a curious person and a curiously attractive one'. Trotsky learned that it was through Vera that the group had come to know Frederick Engels, who died in London in 1895. Lenin told Trotsky that as a writer Vera did not exactly write but 'puts mosaic together'. Between sentences, she:

walked up and down the room slowly, shuffled about in her slippers, smoked constantly hand-made cigarettes and threw the stubs and half-smoked cigarettes in every direction on all the window seats and tables, and scattered ashes over her jacket, hands, manuscripts, tea in the glass, and incidentally her visitor.

When Vera died in 1919, friends discovered that her rooms in Petersburg were horribly cluttered with dirty crockery, ash-trays and books. She seems to have maintained a similarly untidy approach to political discussions. In both formal and informal debates between the comrades, Vera's odd, impulsive manner could be disconcerting. Trotsky observed that it was sometimes hard to follow Zasulich's contributions to political discussions, because, though what she said was relevant, it was sometimes, as we would say, 'out of synch' with the rest of the conversation, seemed inconsistent and came from her own unique perspective.

Vera's approach to writing and discussion were important, and carefully noted by Trotsky, because revolutionaries in exile, like the *Iskra* group, spent a lot of their time writing and debating. Marx, Engels, Trotsky and Lenin were all prolific writers, whose works came out in the form of books, pamphlets, and articles in newspapers and magazines, some of which they set up for themselves. There were also letters, either simply exchanged among the revolutionaries, or smuggled to avoid interception by the authorities, some of which were intended for publication. An example of 'open letters' designed to be widely read would be Lenin's response to the February revolution of 1917, in the form of two letters smuggled into Russia by Alexandra Kollontai in her corset.

It would be possible to write a whole history of the Russian Revolution, its lead-up and aftermath, in terms of the media used to put the message across. The means by which written material in particular was conveyed, either openly or in secret, encoded or not, translated or in the original language, might form an interesting chapter, and there could be another chapter on stormy editorial meetings related to various underground publications.

In Vera Zasulich's time, without widespread telephone systems, radio, television or the internet, the written word was central to politics. Perhaps thousands could attend a speech given by Trotsky, a born orator, but the written word could be circulated among millions. When the communists got their feet under the table in Moscow's Kremlin, they were quick to explore the propaganda possibilities of the then relatively new medium of film. Then it was that the powerful works of the director Sergei Eisenstein had their time of flourishing.

From Trotsky's point of view, Vera Zasulich's 'sharp mind' led her to be sceptical about aspects of Marxism, though she had read and written so much about Marx's ideas and, as we have seen, had even corresponded with the man himself. According to Trotsky, Lenin found Vera too emotional and subjective. She described Lenin, to his face, as a bulldog – a creature that will bite and then hang on like grim death. Lenin was apparently delighted with this characterisation.

In his book on Lenin, Trotsky hinted that one reason why Zasulich drifted away from the centre of politics after the revolutions of 1905 and 1917 was that 'the moral and political foundations of a Russian radical of the 1870s persisted in her, undiminished, to the end'.

As well as having doubts about Marxism in general, Vera was sometimes openly critical of key policies of the *Iskra* group, and at the second congress of the RSDLP in London in 1903 Zasulich and Trotsky joined others in embracing the Menshevik faction, in opposition to Lenin's Bolsheviks. The Mensheviks of this time objected to Lenin's strategy of depending, for the genesis of the coming revolution, on the efforts of ruthless professional revolutionaries, and not so much on the usual political business of spreading the word and trying to influence public opinion. Eventually, Trotsky would cross over to the Bolshevik faction and become, with Lenin, one of the two leading lights of the 1917 revolution.

Back in the early years of the twentieth century, Vera had had doubts about Lenin's approach to revolutionary work, and she was appalled by the 1917 revolution and deeply disillusioned by the new *status quo* that emerged in its aftermath. In 1914 she had joined the Yedinstvo or 'Unity' party of her friend the veteran Russian Marxist Georgi Plekhanov, but as Lenin's Bolsheviks consolidated their power it became clear that Russia was going to become a communist one-party state, not a parliamentary democracy with several alternative parties. Shortly after Plekhanov died in Finland in 1918, the Yedinstvo party was suppressed.

Given her endless smoking and her untidy, absent-minded habits, it is unsurprising that a dangerous fire broke out in Vera's rooms in Petersburg in 1919. This seems to have triggered pneumonia in Zasulich, and she died in May of that year. She was sixty-nine. Although she had taken at least one lover during her life, she had never married or had children.

Trotsky was right to say that Vera Zasulich was a 'curious person'. She was also a contradictory character, in many ways. She briefly became the most famous woman in Europe, yet she was sometimes painfully shy, quiet and withdrawn. Despite her shyness, she often seemed relaxed, even serene in company. Her beliefs had persuaded her to take daring and decisive action, yet she was someone who could happily sit in silence, reading or smoking, alone in a room for days on end. Famous for a violent, potentially murderous act, she later eschewed violence altogether.

Although she grieved for the oppression of the Russian people under the tsars, she herself was from an aristocratic background, and found that she could not thrive in a peasant hut, when she and her comrades 'went to the people' of Ukraine, to try to light the fuse of revolution. Their cover at this time was that they were supposedly running a tea-room from their peasant cabin, but it seems that these radical intellectuals, who had been raised in houses with servants, barely knew how to make tea, let alone bake cakes or run a business.

She lived for years in shared houses with the other comrades in London, Geneva and elsewhere, but Vera Zasulich always seemed to remain detached and self-contained. She may have acquired this way of being herself from her time in solitary confinement, but we should not forget that the attempted murder that put her in prison and also brought her world-wide fame had been very much a solitary act.

Such a detached person cannot easily adjust to marching in step with a crowd of other people, even comrades who share many of her beliefs. It may be that Vera Zasulich could never have fitted in completely with any group, be it a political group, a group of ordinary employees in a workplace, a group of students on the same course, or a family. The other daughters of the Russian revolution who feature in this book also had to weigh their individual instincts, perceptions and needs against those of larger movements.

Trotsky in 1897

Alexandra Kollontai

On Sunday January the twenty-second, 1905, a peaceful procession comprising some fifteen thousand protestors wound its way through the Petersburg snow to the Winter Palace, the tsar's home in the Russian capital. The protestors were led by a good-looking, charismatic young Orthodox priest from Ukraine, Father Georgi Gapon. Known as a friend of working people, in 1904 Gapon had responded to the plight of Russia's poverty-stricken proletariat by founding the Assembly of Russian Workers of St Petersburg. Gapon's Assembly organised highly disruptive strikes involving thousands of workers. Among the demands of the good father's organisation were freedom of speech, a working day limited to eight hours, more democracy in government and an end to the disastrous war Russia was then engaged in, against Japan.

Although Gapon's organisation apparently had no interest in such issues as equal pay for women, it attracted many female members. One of these was the activist Vera Karelina, who was also linked to the St Petersburg League of Struggle for the Emancipation of the Working Class, a group dominated by Vladimir Lenin. Lenin, by the way, had been born in 1870, the same year as both Gapon and Karelina. Vera Karelina became, in effect, Gapon's deputy, and helped to turn his thinking in a more political direction. She also helped to organise the January 1905 march in Petersburg.

Another woman who found that she could associate with Gapon and also be a member of another group was Alexandra Kollontai, who was a couple of years younger than both Karelina and Gapon. Kollontai, the daughter of an aristocratic army general of Ukrainian heritage, joined Lenin's Social Democratic Labour Party in 1899, the year she first encountered Lenin. This was the party that later split into two factions: the Mensheviks and the Bolsheviks.

As a member of Gapon's group, Kollontai trudged through the snow to the Winter Palace with the thousands of other protestors, on that fateful day in January 1905. As well as being peaceful and unarmed, the protest resembled a religious procession, as it was led by a priest, and many of Gapon's followers were carrying religious icons. They were also holding up pictures of the tsar, a semi-divine figure for many believers at the time.

Like one of the demonstrations staged by the British Chartists, the purpose of Gapon's march was to present a petition to the tsar, who had fled the Winter Palace when he got word of the upcoming event. Having reached the palace, the protestors stood for two hours in the snow, before mounted Cossacks charged them, hacking at the crowd with their long swords. The cavalry charge was followed up by machine-gun fire, and soon there were blood and bodies on the snow, over a hundred dead and twice as many injured.

The reactions of the marchers standing near Alexandra Kollontai included utter disbelief and bewilderment. These people thought of the tsar as their guardian, their 'little father' sent by God to look after their interests. Later, both Kollontai and Gapon wrote that, in effect, the Russian emperor had stepped over an important line, and could never turn back. On that day, Kollontai wrote, the tsar 'had killed superstition, and the workers' faith that they could ever achieve justice from him. From then on everything was different and new'.

Both Kollontai and Gapon escaped unhurt: Gapon sheltered in the Petersburg house of the writer Maxim Gorky, confiding in the great man that in his opinion there was now 'no tsar any more, no church, no God'. The disillusioned priest now fled to Geneva, where he made contact with a number of exiled Russian revolutionaries, including Georgi Plekhanov, and our friend Vera Zasulich.

Having abandoned Jesus, Gapon was now ready to embrace Marx, but there were other Russian political exiles who wanted Gapon on their side, for whom Marx was not as important as he was for Zasulich and her associates. The Anarchists and the Socialist Revolutionaries began to court Gapon, not realising that he was also working as an agent for the Russian police. When this became known, the double-agent was hanged by three Socialist Revolutionaries in a cottage outside Petersburg, in April 1906.

Gapon

In terms of potential to bring about lasting change both Father Gapon and the Russian revolution of 1905 had proved to be dead ends. The autocracy that characterised the empire of the tsar, which had sent so many of his subjects into exile, was maintained with brutal suppression, insidious espionage and strict censorship. Kollontai's own father, General Mikhail Domontovich, had fallen foul of the censor in the 1880s, when his book *An Overview of the Russian-Turkish War of 1877-1878* had been suppressed and confiscated.

Alexandra herself played a two-year game of cat and mouse with the Russian police after she published a pamphlet called *Finland and Socialism* in 1906. A collection of her articles on the political situation in Finland, the pamphlet was intended to inspire the Finns to cast off the yoke of Russian rule and become an independent country. In those days, Russian tsars were also made dukes of Finland when they were made emperor: Finland was ruled as a duchy. Something similar still happens in the UK, where the Prince of Wales, the heir to the throne, is always also the Duke of Cornwall, and is traditionally referred to as 'the Duke' in that county. As a direct attack on the authority of the tsar in his duchy of Finland, Kollontai's *Finland and Socialism* meant that there was soon a warrant out for the arrest of the author. Another warrant was issued in 1908, provoked by her call for an armed uprising.

Kollontai was no doubt concerned with Finland partly because she had the country in her blood. Her mother, also an Alexandra, was the daughter of a Finn who had been born a serf but had won his freedom even before the liberation of the serfs in 1861. He had then gone on to make a fortune in the timber industry. The first Alexandra's famous daughter grew up speaking Finnish to the servants at the estate her mother had inherited from her own father, Kollontai's grandfather, Alexander Masalina. When she was not in Finland, the little girl was in Petersburg.

Kollontai's mother ran the family timber business from the Finnish estate, and the family was unusual in other ways as well. The first Alexandra had been a married woman with three children when she fell in love with Kollontai's father, and the pair had gone through the then tortuous, prolonged process of procuring a divorce for Kollontai's mother, something that was almost unheard of at the time.

Growing up in the house of a serious businesswoman, Kollontai had the example of a strong, self-reliant mother always before her eyes. The family also believed in educating their three girls to the highest possible standard, employing carefully-chosen tutors and not hesitating to send them abroad to improve their education. Alexandra proved to be an apt student, with a particularly strong talent for acquiring new languages.

Kollontai's third step-sibling, a boy, stayed with his father, Kollontai's mother's first husband.

Alexandra Kollontai went into exile in 1908, after two years of avoiding arrest. Her exile was not her first extended trip abroad. As a young woman her parents had sent her west in the hope that she would forget her suitor, a hard-up student of engineering called Vladimir Kollontai. In 1898 she had gone to Zurich to study economics, although by this time she had already been married for four years to Kollontai, and had borne a child by him, Mikhail (or Misha) in 1894. The boy was left with her parents when she departed for Switzerland.

In Zurich, Kollontai studied under Professor Heinrich Herkner, but she disagreed with his political stance. While Kollontai and the 'orthodox' Marxists believed that a revolution was necessary to bring in a socialist world, Herkner and his fellow 'revisionists' wanted to avoid the chaos of revolution and bring about socialism by more peaceful means. Herkner even sent Kollontai to visit his British Fabian friends Sydney and Beatrice Webb, to listen to their arguments, but the Russian visitor to London was not convinced.

Though her relationship with her first husband was not to last – she began divorce proceedings on her return from Zurich – being married, albeit briefly, to an engineer had opened her eyes to new aspects of life in the empire of the tsar, and had helped her define her own political stance. In 1896, visiting a cotton-mill in Narva, Estonia which Vladimir and a small team were planning to improve by, for instance, installing a ventilation system with filters to strain the deadly cotton dust out of the air, Kollontai got a sense of the terrible conditions many worked in. She learned that cotton in the lungs led to respiratory problems that shortened young lives, and she even found a dead baby on the floor of one of the workers' dorms.

According to her short autobiography, Vladimir and the engineers put their hope in improvements in technology to raise the standard of living of the hard-working proletariat. His wife came to believe that revolutionary change was needed, that the workers themselves should own and run what the Marxists termed 'the means of production'.

After 1908 Kollontai became a brilliant addition to the large Russian ex-pat community in western Europe. She had been reading left-wing literature, some of it illegal in Russia, for years, and had been active in left-wing politics and trade unionism before, during and after her involvement with Gapon's ill-fated movement. A particular focus of her political work was the task of keeping the plight and rights of women as much as possible before the eyes of her male fellow-revolutionaries. There was serious resistance to some of this from Kollontai's Social Democratic comrades, and at times she must have felt that she was fighting both the tsar and her own people.

Kollontai also opposed the existing feminist movement in Russia, which she characterised as groups of middle- and upper-class women campaigning for their own liberation, but paying scant regard to the oppression of their working-class sisters. Her last significant act before escaping into exile in 1908 was to help coordinate a group of women workers whom she wanted to disrupt a feminist conference in Petersburg.

Kollontai's attitude to the 1908 All-Russian Congress of Women that her team had tried to disrupt was embodied in her book *The Social Basis of the Woman Question*, in which she also set out some of her ideas about how a revolution in attitudes to love and sex might contribute to the liberation of women. She seems to have pictured as the future socialist ideal a world where women would not feel obliged to get married and have children just to live with a lover, have sex and enjoy male company.

'Free love' outside marriage would be a mark of a woman's independence, but Kollontai was careful to distinguish between that kind of equal, consensual extra-marital sex and the activities of powerful, promiscuous men who took advantage of vulnerable women over whom they had power. She wrote of men who ran factories and offices and coerced their female employees. What Kollontai saw as the grim realities of contemporary sex and marriage were, to her, inevitable given the wretched way that work and economics were organised under capitalism. Only a revolution that gave birth to a new context could bring about true equality and liberation.

Such opinions, which seemed to be anti-marriage but were actually just against the wrong kind of oppressive, unequal marriage, were shocking to many of Kollontai's contemporaries in the early years of the twentieth century, when, in many circles, discussion of such subjects as sex and birth-control was taboo. Kollontai had read Freud on sex, and also Havelock Ellis, the white-bearded English writer on such matters. Many of Kollontai's contemporaries would have categorised Ellis's works as obscene pornography, and the mention of his writings could still elicit embarrassed titters, at least in his home country, late into the twentieth century.

Another author Kollontai turned to was the Austrian Grete Meisel-Hess, whose 1909 book *The Sexual Crisis* she reviewed in 1911. Like Kollontai, Meisel-Hess believed that conventional bourgeois marriages were essentially unhealthy and could even lead to the 'degeneration' of the race and the rise and increase of prostitution. Among her solutions was what a 1972 translation of Kollontai's review renders as 'game-love'. In the absence of a deep, abiding love-connection, people should turn to less serious forms of erotic engagement. This sounds remarkably like the modern idea of 'friends with benefits' where a relationship is based on friendship and sex, but love is not supposed to come into it.

Kollontai had long been familiar with the theories of Marx, as well as the ideas of Freud, Ellis and Grete Meisel-Hess, and in exile she was able to meet, or renew her acquaintance with, thinkers who were living links to the great man himself. These included the philosopher Karl Kautsky, who had been a close friend of Marx's comrade Frederick Engels; the German Marxist Rosa Luxemburg, and the socialist Karl Liebknecht, whose father Wilhelm had known both Marx and Engels.

Kollontai spent most of her time in exile before the Great War in Berlin, where she quickly joined the German socialist party. Despite her comrades' reservations about some of her views, she became an active and useful contributor to the cause of socialism in the West. She was willing to travel widely, and was able to give rousing speeches in English, French and German, as well as Russian.

She addressed rioters and strikers as well as political meetings, but while she seemed to be keen to throw a burning match into the tinder-box that was European politics and industrial relations at the time, many of her more cautious comrades were as reluctant as her old tutor Heinrich Herkner had been to actually ignite a revolution. The horrific aftermath of the failed 1905 revolution in Russia gave them the jitters.

Among the comrades who agreed with Kollontai's more radical approach were Luxemburg, Liebknecht, and Clara Zetkin, the last a formidable German equivalent of Kollontai herself. At the second Conference of Working Women in Copenhagen in 1910, Zetkin, a member of the German Social Democratic Party, proposed the idea of an international day for working women. According to an article published by Kollontai in 1920, the idea had first cropped up in the United States the previous year, when socialist working women 'organized huge demonstrations and meetings all over the country demanding political rights . . . the initiative on organizing a woman's day thus belongs to the working women of America'.

In the same article, published in Moscow, Kollontai wrote about the widespread success of the first Women's Day in 1911, when 'Germany and Austria . . . was one seething, trembling sea of women. Meetings were organized everywhere – in the small towns and even in the villages halls were packed so full that they had to ask male workers to give up their places for the women. This was certainly the first show of militancy by the working woman. Men stayed at home with their children for a change, and their wives, the captive housewives, went to meetings' (trans. Alix Holt, 1972).

The day is still marked on March the eighth in many parts of the world, though many forget its left-wing origins. Both before and after the revolution of 1917, Kollontai was keen to see International Women's Day marked in Russia. In her article she insists, however, that many of the burdens women had borne throughout history could soon be banished from Soviet Russia, if male and female workers cooperated 'to put right Russia's shattered economy', to get the transport system on its feet again and help everyone to 'get the bread and firewood they desperately need'.

Despite the success International Women's Day had enjoyed in its first years, the advent of the Great War meant that the day in 1915 and 1916 'was a feeble affair'. Women who supported the Bolsheviks' stance on the war tried but failed to mount anti-war demonstrations on the day, but were stymied by the widespread support for the war even among other socialists. Though the revolution that turned Kollontai into perhaps the most powerful woman in Russia was born out of the chaos of the war, in many places 1914 meant the shelving of the socialist agenda and the grim embrace of patriotism, nationalism and militarism.

Kollontai's 1915 article *Who Needs the War?* is a coherent and compelling statement of the Bolshevik position on the conflict, and includes some classic pacifist arguments that are not necessarily political at all. It begins with an evocation of what civilians and survivors were likely to see in towns, cities and villages in Russia and elsewhere at the time: 'the armless, the legless, the blind, the deaf, the mutilated . . . they were brought back to the infirmaries half dead, crippled . . .' (trans. Cynthia Carlile, 1984). One is reminded of the works of the German painter Otto Dix (1891-1969), who had fought in the war and whose picture *War Cripples* (1920) shows men still in uniform and adorned with medals, but missing arms, legs, eyes and parts of faces.

'War cripples' are heroes according to some, Kollontai asserts, but when the hero comes home to his native village or town, he cannot believe his eyes: in place of respect and joy he finds fresh sufferings and disillusionment. The author tells us that the Russian tsar's pension, awarded to such veterans, 'would hardly pay for one boot for the one leg remaining'.

Kollontai's emphasis on the maimed and blinded is good rhetoric: even in the midst of a war that may have killed more than twenty million, over half of them civilians, it was hard for the living to comprehend death, and of course the dead are always buried or otherwise hidden away. But grim processions limping through the streets to 'join the beggars on the church porch' are harder to ignore.

And what were these home-coming heroes fighting for? Kollontai asserts that if you ask them 'they will not tell you, they will not answer, because they themselves do not really know'. Even now, with the benefit of hindsight, and innumerable books and screen documentaries about the Great War, many people would struggle to explain what the war was actually about.

In her widely-read and translated *Who Needs the War?* Kollontai went through several of the most popular justifications for the war and showed them all to be specious, even delusional. Did the Germans really think they were saving the Russians by fighting them? Did the Russians really think they were saving the Germans?

The Bolshevik view of the war was that thousands of young workers had been convinced that they should try to kill thousands of brother-workers who happened to be from another country. The real enemy was not 'foreign' workers but the aristocracy and bourgeoisie of these countries, and the real war was a class war between them and the workers they had oppressed for centuries. In her article, Kollontai points out how artificial these opposing countries were in the first place. The Great War was really a clash of empires and not just countries, and the subjects or citizens of these countries, in uniform or in civvies, were extremely diverse. This meant that between 1914 and 1918 Russian Poles ended up fighting against Poles from further west, Russian Orthodox Christians fought people of the same faith, and even Muslims were fighting Muslims.

That the war was a clash of empires was not lost on Lenin. In the first of the two so-called *Letters From Afar* that he wrote, and which Kollontai smuggled into Russia in her corset after the February revolution of 1917, Vladimir Iliich referred to 'the imperialist world war' that had 'engendered . . . the first stage of the first revolution'. He was clear that the imperial powers were not merely fighting over land in Europe, but over the right to continue with 'the plunder of foreign countries and the strangling of small nations, for financial world supremacy and the division and redivision of colonies' (trans. Levin, Fineberg et al, 1964).

Lenin and Kollontai's critiques of the war may have fallen on deaf ears if the approach to it, on the Russian side, had not been so utterly hopeless. As had happened during the Russo-Japanese war of 1904-5, the incompetence and corruption of the Russians in charge of the conduct of the war led to widespread frustration, disillusionment, embarrassment, and despair.

The tsar himself, Nicholas II, had well and truly set himself up for a fall by taking personal charge of his country's war effort in 1915. In an unfinished article translated by Cathy Porter as *Who Needs the Tsar and Can We Do Without Him?* Kollontai ridiculed the emperor himself and the whole concept of monarchy, and painted a picture of the tsar visiting battlefields ('not the front line, perish the thought') where his presence causes 'the hearts of many in their grey army coats [to] beat faster, and they long to show off their valour to him' (Porter, *Alexandra Kollontai: Writings from the Struggle*, 2020).

Although many celebrations marking International Women's Day were disappointing amid the distractions of the Great War, in Russia women marking the day played a crucial role in the February Revolution of 1917. The women involved began their 'celebrations' a day early, on the seventh of March. After so many years of war, with its tragedies and privations, they had nothing to celebrate. They marked the occasion with days of strikes, protests and even old-fashioned Luddite activities, such as smashing up factory equipment.

All this happened against a background of widespread strikes, riots, and mutinies among and mass desertions from the armed forces. The women's protests snowballed – the existing unrest formed the snow further down the hill, that coalesced round the core of their activity. As things escalated, the tsar abdicated on the fifteenth of March 1917, and Russia found itself with a Provisional Government and a People's Soviet, sharing power.

Kollontai first read the news of the revolution in someone else's newspaper, peering over the shoulder of a fellow-passenger, on a tram trundling into the Norwegian town of Holmenkollen, then her place of exile. As had happened in 1905, the revolution had taken the exiled revolutionaries by surprise. Further news, for instance of the tsar's abdication, engendered key questions in the hot heads of the Russian exiles in Norway, and their Norwegian comrades. Would the tsar return as part of a constitutional monarchy? Would one of his relatives fight to reinstate the Romanov dynasty, that had ruled Russia for three hundred years? What role would the Bolsheviks play in the coming events? What did Lenin know or think, in exile in Switzerland? Would the revolution mean that Russia could exit the war? Would the new government grant women more rights, and include women in the business of running the country?

As we know, under a general amnesty for political exiles, Kollontai was able to return to Russia, with two crucial letters from Lenin hidden in her corset. While some Bolsheviks who were already there in Petersburg, such as Joseph Stalin, were ready to compromise with the Provisional Government, Lenin did not trust Alexander Kerensky, its leader, and wanted to overthrow him, having first 'Bolshevised' the People's Soviet. Lenin famously arrived at Petersburg's Finland Station on the sixteenth of April 1917, where he was greeted by a huge, rapturous crowd, in the midst of which was Alexandra Kollontai carrying a bunch of flowers.

The Bolsheviks made their headquarters in Petersburg's Smolny Institute, once a kind of finishing-school for aristocratic Russian girls. There, in grand ballrooms under opulent chandeliers, half-starved, louse-infested soldiers from the front would drink cabbage soup in company with left-leaning intellectuals like Kollontai and Trotsky, the latter of whom had thrown in his lot with the Bolsheviks in August 1917.

The process of Bolshevising Russia involved persuasion, propaganda and brute force. Since so many Russians were in uniform at the time, it was particularly important to win servicemen over to the Bolshevik cause. Kollontai spoke to rooms packed with soldiers, and also turned her attention to the sailors posted in two naval bases, at

Kronstadt on Kotlin Island off Petersburg, and Helsinki on the Finnish coast (then known as Helsingfors). The sailors at Kronstadt were already pretty solidly Bolshevik, but at Helsingfors the party of Lenin and Kollontai was in the minority. The tars there had, however, elected a Bolshevik, Pavel Dybenko, as the head of *Tsentrobalt*, a committee sitting above other sailors' committees in the Baltic fleet.

Dybenko

Like Lenin, Dybenko also distrusted Kerensky, and there is even a story that he threw the leader of the Provisional Government overboard from a naval ship. While Dybenko, with Kollontai's help, was persuading the Baltic sailors to get into bed, figuratively, with the Bolsheviks, Kollontai was literally getting into bed with him. Soon they were married, in one of the first of a new type of secular 'red' weddings. (When Trotsky married his first wife in 1899, there had been no such thing as a secular wedding in Russia, so the pair were spliced by a rabbi.)

Dybenko and Kollontai made an odd couple. She was forty-five; he was twenty-eight. Whereas she was derived, at least on one side, from Russian nobility, his forebears were Ukrainian peasants. She was an intellectual with a command of several languages, whereas he struggled to write well and had a limited vocabulary. Lenin had plenty of reasons to suspect the marriage, and he was not silent on the subject. The marriage may have made perfect sense to Kollontai when she looked at her dashing, handsome young partner, but the politest thing that can be said about Pavel's character is that it was that of a dangerously unstable adventurer.

Kollontai's second husband was forever making audacious choices, such as marrying an older woman and throwing Kerensky overboard. Sometimes these choices paid off handsomely; at other times they got him into deep trouble. But he had the luck of the devil, and a wife who acquired a lot of influence when her Bolshevik party gained control of Russia's tottering empire. Kollontai would fight Pavel's corner and ensure a steady flow of second chances and glittering opportunities.

His new wife was useful to Dybenko in other ways: when he had to pass exams, she wrote his assignments for him. She also wrote books that were published under his name, and came up with ideas that he passed off as his own.

In 1917 Dybenko, like Kollontai, became one of the fourteen members of Lenin's first 'cabinet', the Council of People's Commissars. He was in charge of naval affairs. She was the only woman, and was appointed People's Commissar of Social Welfare. The last of these original commissars to die was Joseph Stalin, Commissar of Nationalities in Lenin's first cabinet, who ended his reign of terror in 1953. Kollontai had died in Moscow in the previous year. Many of the others, including Dybenko, were executed on Stalin's orders in the nineteen-thirties. Trotsky, originally Commissar for Foreign Affairs, was assassinated on Stalin's orders in Mexico in 1940.

Various foreign nations reacted with alarm to the news that the Bolsheviks, who would re-name themselves the communists in 1918, had gained control in Petersburg and were ruling through a cabinet headed by Lenin. Russia was invaded from several different directions, and soon a complex civil war descended on a people already shattered by the Great War. Among Russia's new enemies were the British, the French and the Americans, and the so-called White Russians; home-grown anti-Bolsheviks.

The situation was particularly chaotic in Ukraine, where anarchist and Ukrainian nationalist elements added to the mix. In 1919, Lenin sent Kollontai's second husband to Ukraine, partly because of his Ukrainian surname and background. There his forces ran riot, carrying out massacres and executions, and looting and robbing wherever they could. In April Dybenko invaded Crimea, right against his orders, and founded his own Crimean Soviet Socialist Republic, inviting both Kollontai and Lenin's brother Dmitry Ulianov to help him rule it. His personal republic only lasted a few months.

In August 1917, when Trotsky officially joined the Bolsheviks, the American reporter Louise Bryant (our last daughter of the revolution) and her husband Jack Reed set off for Russia to cover events. For English readers, Reed's book *Ten Days That Shook the World* is an engrossing, epic eye-witness account of the rise of the Bolsheviks in Petersburg; but Bryant's book *Six Red Months in Russia*, covering almost the same period, is just as important, if less well-known. It offers a more human side-light on things, and features in particular interviews with leading women in Russia at the time.

Bryant's account of Alexandra Kollontai begins with a pen-portrait of the woman she replaced, the Countess Sofia Panina, Vice Minister of State for both Welfare and Education, under Kerensky's Provisional Government. Trying, perhaps, to give her American readers something familiar to latch onto, Bryant observed that the countess looked like the U.S. suffragist Jane Addams. Bryant also contrasted the countess with 'plain citizen' Kollontai, neglecting to mention the latter's aristocratic ancestry. By the time Bryant met the two women, they were bitter enemies.

Despite (or perhaps partly because of) her status as a nob, the Bolsheviks imprisoned Panina in Petersburg's historic Peter and Paul fortress, where she received her American visitor in her book-lined cell. Bryant noted that the Provisional Government had imprisoned Kollontai in the same fortress just a short time earlier. Lenin's government arrested and tried Panina for, as they saw it, embezzling ninety thousand roubles of state money. The countess herself insisted that she was holding on to this money until the long longed-for Constituent Assembly should be elected and come to power in Russia.

Panina was evidently unable to accept the authority of the new Bolshevik rulers. When the Constituent Assembly finally met in January 1918, Lenin's government shut it down after just a few hours. A month later, Louise Bryant left Russia and returned to the United States. As for the countess, she never did give up her roubles: she was, however, released from prison because her wealthy friends paid off the Bolsheviks.

Her retention of the money, and other behaviour of the middle-aged prisoner, was regarded by Louise Bryant as sabotage. Sabotage was a real problem for Panina's successor, Alexandra Kollontai, who put a great deal of effort into reforming and refurbishing a care centre for pregnant women and new mothers, only to see it burned down by arsonists.

It is evident from the beginning of Bryant's account of her friend Kollontai in *Six Red Months* that the plight of Russia's destitute and often maimed war veterans was a priority for her, despite her work for mothers and babies, and other groups. She had of course written about these poor men and their families in her 1915 article *Who Needs the War?* As a commissar, her enthusiasm for their cause got her into deep trouble. According to Kollontai herself, writing in 1927, while her beloved veterans were sleeping in the streets, Petersburg's Alexander Nevsky monastery was stuffed with food and firewood (the historic monastery can still be seen on Petersburg's Nevsky Prospect, the street where Vera Zasulich's assassination attempt took place). In January 1918 Kollontai set about trying to turn the complex, which had been founded by Peter the Great himself, into something like a Russian version of England's celebrated Royal Hospital in Chelsea, a home for veterans.

Several aspects of *God's Business With the Monks*, the commissar's own account of this unfortunate affair, smell distinctly fishy. Since she may not have gone anywhere near the monastery at the time, her information was probably second-hand, filtered through the minds of her comrades, who may have wanted to put a positive spin on events. Can we believe that as soon as the Bolsheviks rocked up at the gates, the monastic novices began to denounce the monks, their superiors, as oppressors? This certainly seems convenient from the Bolshevik point of view, since they could claim that they had discovered a previously unsuspected class conflict in the heart of Russia's capital.

Despite the alleged help and agreement of the novices (the proletariat in this context) the monks themselves would not consent to giving up their home to Kollontai's war veterans, so she called on her husband Pavel Dybenko to take the place by force. As Dybenko's sailors approached, the monks rang a bell, which summoned armed supporters of the monks from the surrounding community. There was a stand-off between the monks and the sailors; in the end, six lay dead.

His wife was not the only one who called on Dybenko when strong-arm tactics were needed. Pavel was a major player in the notorious suppression of the Kronstadt naval rebellion in March 1921. The sailors at the base had grown tired of the tyranny of the new communist government, and the broken state of their country, which left many starving and destitute. On the orders of Trotsky, the base was attacked by Red Army troops who surged across the ice that linked the island to the mainland in the winter months. Over two thousand were killed, and a similar number of rebels was later executed.

The whole unfortunate affair of the monastery formed a crack in Kollontai's relationship with Lenin, which had previously been so close and fruitful. He knew that, given the devotion many still felt towards the Orthodox Church, one way the Bolsheviks could alienate the people would be by attacking its priests and monks. The rift between Kollontai and Lenin widened further when, like several members of the latter's first cabinet, Alexandra found that she could not agree to the terms of the Treaty of Brest-Litovsk, signed in March 1918. The Treaty got Russia out of the Great War, but at the cost of huge tracts of the old tsarist empire, including Ukraine and Finland. As one of the so-called 'Left Communists', Kollontai felt obliged to resign as commissar.

Alexandra was, however, far too useful to the cause to remain away from the centre of power for very long. With the civil war still grinding on, she wrote, spoke and travelled tirelessly, sometimes riding on the famous 'agit-trains' and agit-steamers. The agit-trains were festooned with red flags, their carriages painted with revolutionary images and slogans. Often they had printing-presses on board, and distributed huge quantities of pro-Russian, pro-communist propaganda. Many Russians in far-away places experienced cinema for the first time on these trains, and watched revolutionary plays staged by travelling companies of actors.

Kollontai worked hard establishing women's groups, and in 1919 she became one of the founders of the *Zhenotdel*, a body designed to fight for the women's rights that she and others had worked to write into the Russian communist programme. Alexandra herself had clashed with Lenin too many times to be considered for the post of head of the *Zhenotdel*: this went to her friend Inessa Armand, who, as we will see, may have been Lenin's mistress. When Armand died of cholera in September 1920, Kollontai took over.

Although figures like Lenin paid lip-service to Kollontai's ideas about women's power and liberation, such issues had been repeatedly side-lined by male members of the Party, and the *Zhenotdel*'s ideas were ignored, if not ridiculed. Worse, Kollontai's insistence on the role of sex in renewing the family and women's lives was often pointed to as an example of decadence and immorality. Against this background of disapproval, and in the prevailing atmosphere of panic, chaos and failure, Kollontai's work on enlightened new legislation relating to, for instance, abortion seemed to make little impression. At times she must have felt like a woman trying to pick out a tune on a broken balalaika in the middle of a cacophonous bombardment.

Despite her gruelling, frustrating workload as head of the *Zhenotdel,* Kollontai still found time to find fault with the progress of the revolution. Having once been one of the Left Communists who lined up against the Brest-Litovsk treaty, she now spoke for the Workers' Opposition, for instance in a sort of manifesto for the group that she penned in 1921. Like the sailors at Kronstadt who had been so mercilessly knocked down by Dybenko and his troops, the members of the Workers' Opposition were impatient with the state of things after the end of the Great War and the civil war, and several years of Bolshevik rule.

Unemployment, starvation and homelessness were widespread, Russia was being battered by horrendous epidemics, including of sexually transmitted diseases, and the workers who had once been downtrodden under capitalist bosses now found themselves being exploited by bureaucrats and 'specialists'. In some cases the people running the factories were the same people who had run them before, but with new job-titles. The people in charge, including party officials, were living rather better than the destitute proletariat, and important infrastructure, including transport and health-care, was still shattered.

The Bolsheviks tried to breathe new life into the ailing Russian economy by introducing the New Economic Policy (or 'NEP') in March 1921, but in the view of members of the Workers' Opposition the new approach just made the situation worse. The NEP was supposed to temporarily re-introduce capitalist ways of doing things into areas of the Russian economy, a step which seemed to some to be a betrayal of the original principles of the revolution, which had promised collectivisation, nationalisation and workers' control of the means of production.

While highly visible figures like Lenin, Trotsky and Kollontai were engaging in very public disputes about policy, the still relatively obscure figure of Joseph Stalin was working slowly and quietly behind the scenes, assembling power to himself. In this ominous endeavour, he was aided by illnesses that put both Lenin and Trotsky out of action for long periods, and by Lenin's death in 1924, at the age of fifty-three. By

1922, when Stalin was made General Secretary of the Communist Party of the Soviet Union, the Georgian was already powerful enough to be the man who sent Kollontai to Norway, as a new member of the modest Russian trade delegation in Oslo.

Although this posting was partly just a way for Stalin to get the sometimes highly critical Kollontai out of the country, she was a good fit for the role of representative for the Russians in Norway (she could not be an ambassador, as Norway had not yet recognised the Russian Bolshevik government). Alexandra knew many languages, had travelled widely, had many international connections, and already knew Norway well. She quickly got down to work, despite the wild stories that were circulating about her in the local press. Was she a cold-hearted terrorist assassin, or perhaps a louche *femme fatale*? By this time, she was divorced from Dybenko. As well as working as a member of the Soviet trade delegation, Kollontai renewed her acquaintance with the town of Holmenkollen, hiked and climbed in the hills around Oslo, and amused her Norwegian hosts with her terrible skiing.

She also masterminded a scheme whereby Russian wheat could be traded for Norwegian herring, and was also responsible for an important business deal whereby Russian cargo ships would be used to transport Norwegian wood to European buyers. She also negotiated effectively to restore Russia's rights on the island of Spitsbergen, to the north of Norway.

These deals were consistent with Kollontai's role as an agent of Russia trying to encourage trade between her home country and Norway, but the aim of normalising relations between the two countries was always in the back of her mind. In September of 1924 she became a full Russian ambassador to Norway, and formally presented her credentials to the Norwegian king. She therefore became the first female ambassador in the history of diplomacy. By this time, the Norwegians were treating her with respect, and lurid rumours about her character and behaviour were no longer appearing in the Norwegian press.

Still with time on her hands, Kollontai turned to writing fiction during her 'diplomatic exile', something she had dabbled in before, but in the earlier phases of her life the writing of pertinent reports and propaganda books and pamphlets must have seemed more useful to the cause.

Not that the issues raised in Kollontai's two novels were not relevant to the struggle, as they still are. The eponymous heroine of her 1923 novel *Vasilisa Malygina* faces problems that are still faced by many working women (English editions are sometimes titled *The Love of Worker Bees*). Work means that Vasilisa has little time for her husband Vladimir, and the couple even have to live apart for long stretches. When they are living together in her tiny attic room, 'Vasya' has to put up with his complaints about the food she serves him, and the fact that, though he is officially living at home, she still hardly sees him.

Vladimir is a loud-mouth with a tendency to get into trouble, and sometimes he doesn't do any work at all. Vasya is acutely aware that he is handsome while she is rather plain and anaemic, and that he runs after other women. Meanwhile she is often too tired to satisfy him sexually herself. To add insult to injury, her husband does not hesitate to criticise her appearance and her dress-sense. During the revolution, Vasya had grown accustomed to not caring at all about her looks or how she dressed.

A problem with Kollontai's novel is that the heroine is too saintly and down-trodden to allow the average reader to identify with her. She always seems to do the right thing. Kollontai might have made the novel richer if she had given Vasya a few faults, to humanise her: a liking for drink, perhaps, or a tendency to get into fights.

Vasya is under pressure not just from her difficult husband but because of conditions in post-revolutionary Russia, which Kollontai depicts with surprising frankness. The advent of the aforementioned NEP or New Economic Policy means that much that was once free now has to be paid for, and that a new class of exploiters is suddenly creaming off much of the wealth. Now a successful businessman, Vladimir insists that Vasya give up her valuable work and become an idle housewife in a new town. Suddenly she is expected to host swanky dinners where the guests are the kinds of people my grandmother would have called 'shysters'.

One of the dodgy businessmen with whom Vladimir spends too much of his time is sugar-daddy to a beautiful but vulnerable women called Nina, who, it turns out, is also Vladimir's mistress.

Though the powerful Party (meaning the Communist Party) is still trying to enforce rather puritanical proletarian ways of living, the new NEP people are going around in silks and fine furs. Many citizens are confused as to how to live and how to avoid being censured by Party officials. Meanwhile it is all too easy for anyone to denounce anyone else on political grounds.

The situation is reminiscent of the hero's predicament in Franz Kafka's novel *The Trial*, which was completed in 1915 but not published until 1925. The hero, Josef K, is accused of some dreadful crime, but nightmarish bureaucracy means that he is never told exactly what he is supposed to have done. Stultifying bureaucracy is also a feature of *Vasilisa Malygina,* where people have to wait for hours just for a short interview with a local Party official.

Frustrated by life as a sort of suburban housewife, living with a husband who is obsessed with another woman, Vasya decides to go home and go it alone, though she is now pregnant. Because her 'marriage' was never formalised, the field is now clear for Nina. Vasya's decision to become a single mum is brave and modern: in many communities, such a choice would still attract censure. She hopes that her child will be the child of herself and her comrades, thriving in a nursery that she plans to set up.

One similarity between the heroines of both *Vasilisa Malygina* and Kollontai's other novel *A Great Love*, also first published in 1923, is that they both think that their work is important. In this they contrast with many women juggling work and home today, whose work often seems pointless, alienating, demeaning and insecure.

In the UK at the moment (in 2024) the women who do many of the most important jobs, such as the teachers, doctors, nurses and care-workers, are routinely overworked and underpaid. Miserly cuts in all worthwhile public services mean that their roles are often so over-stretched and under-resourced that it is impossible to provide an adequate service. The result for the employee is burn-out, disillusionment, cynicism and a sense of hopelessness.

Though Natasha, the heroine of *A Great Love*, is ultimately convinced that her work for the Party is worthwhile, she feels undermined by the fact that her married lover Semyon does not take her job seriously. A deeply selfish man, he really sees his mistress only in terms of her link to him, not as an important person in herself. He is undoubtedly important, as he is a leader in the Party which, at the start of the novel, is not in power. The pair are part of the diaspora of Russian leftists in the West, before the revolution of 1917.

This makes the cast of characters in *A Great Love* very different from that in Kollontai's other novel, *Vasilisa Malygina*. Natasha, Semyon and the others are forever drifting around Europe, attending international conferences and looking for a place to settle until the local government takes against the idea of foreign revolutionaries renting local flats, riding buses and using libraries. The novel may be partly based on Kollontai's own experience with married lovers during her time in the West before 1917, but its relevance to the relationship between Lenin and his fellow revolutionary Inessa Armand is what has given it a degree of notoriety. Armand was, of course, Kollontai's fellow-worker in the *Zhenotdel*.

Four years younger than Lenin, Armand probably met the great man soon after she escaped from internal exile at Mezen in Northern Russia and joined the Russian diaspora in Western Europe. She soon became an indispensable assistant to Vladimir Iliich, and often lived very close to him and his wife Nadezhda Krupskaya. She and Krupskaya seem to have been good friends, and Inessa got on particularly well with Krupskaya's mother Yelizaveta, who lived with her daughter and son-in-law.

By this time Armand, who was in her mid thirties, had been married twice and borne five children fathered by two different men (who were brothers, as it happens). She had a free-and-easy attitude to sex, but whether she actually went to bed with Lenin, as Kollontai's Natasha does with her Semyon, is still unclear. Kollontai was of course also part of the Russian revolutionary diaspora, knew Armand and Lenin well, and often worked very closely with the latter herself.

Inessa Armand

If the character of Semyon in *A Great Love* is supposed to be Lenin, it is not a flattering portrait. One symptom of his selfishness and egotism is that he is a bad lover who comes on strong in bed and leaves Natasha feeling unsatisfied and abused (to make details like this clear in a novel written a century ago was bold of Kollontai). It is clear from the start of the novel that Natasha and Semyon have repeatedly broken up, but that she repeatedly agrees when he wants to get together again.

Kollontai's fiction attracted a lot of attention and proved popular, but it also re-enforced her image as a woman who was prepared to be outspoken about sex, and about failings in the new society in Russia.

Despite her success as Russia's representative in Norway, both in post and on various trips to Moscow Kollontai felt the severe wind-chill of Stalin's paranoid, autocratic approach to government. She was subjected to prolonged, intrusive interrogations at the hands of the Party's Control Commission, and her name was repeatedly dragged through the mud in *Pravda* and other parts of the Russian press. She had become one of the so-called 'Old Bolsheviks' whom Stalin would dearly love to have got rid of, but despite her tarnished reputation she was still too popular and well-known for the monstrous Georgian to act against her directly.

Stalin had developed a tactic of sending such enemies away on diplomatic missions to places that were likely to damage their health. In her 1980 biography of Kollontai, Cathy Porter suggests that the writer Maxim Gorky died of pneumonia in 1936, at the age of sixty-eight, because he had been sent to Crimea, then forced to return to the much colder climate of Moscow (other sources suggest that Gorky may have been poisoned). In Kollontai's case, Stalin suggested a diplomatic transfer to Mexico City, which is very hot and dry, and over seventeen thousand feet above sea level, making it a dangerous place for a woman like Alexandra, who had a weak heart and high blood pressure.

Fourteen years after Kollontai set off for Mexico City, the place proved fatal for the exiled fugitive Leon Trotsky, who was assassinated by a Stalinist agent there in 1940. When she reached Mexico after a tortuous journey, Kollontai met the Mexican artist Diego Rivera: in Mexico City, Trotsky and his wife would live for a while with Rivera and his own wife, the iconic Frida Kahlo.

In Mexico City, the capital of that country 'so far from heaven, but so close to the United States', Kollontai found herself struggling for breath. A doctor assured her that she would soon acclimatise to the altitude, but she never did. At times she was obliged, for the sake of her health, to take breaks outside the city, but the politics of Mexico at the time was extremely volatile, and her posting was hardly relaxing. She returned to Russia in 1927, with several Mexican paintings, including one of Rivera's, among her souvenirs.

She was sent back to Oslo, where she found that she was expected to supervise the refurbishment of the old tsarist embassy. This she found utterly tedious, and she reflected that if she had been a male ambassador, she may at least have had a wife who could have taken such jobs in hand. But in the damp, cold Norwegian climate she felt healthier, and visitors were astonished by the vigorous way she clambered over rocks and up snow-covered hills.

In 1930 Kollontai was transferred to Sweden, where anti-Russian and anti-communist feeling meant that she had a frosty reception at first. But her geniality and her genius for networking soon broke down the barriers, and she was able to build personal, political, industrial and financial bridges. She even managed to persuade the Swedes to repatriate Russian gold that Kerensky, the head of the old Provisional Government, had salted away in Swedish banks. Everyone was welcome at the friendly dinners that were eaten around a big table at Kollontai's Russian embassy in Stockholm, where the whole household, including the cooks and chauffeurs, shared in the meal.

While Kollontai had struggled to breathe in Mexico City, her native Russia was suffocating in the grip of Joseph Stalin, who was now emerging as one of history's deadliest dictators. His numerous purges of people he imagined might oppose him took in many different ranks of Russians. In 1938, when it was the army's turn, Alexandra's ex-husband Pavel Dybenko was tried in secret, with Stalin himself looking on. He was told he would be put in charge of the timber industry in the Urals. He dutifully hurried there to take up his new post, but was shot dead on arrival.

At times in Norway and Sweden the frenetic Kollontai had found things a little dull, but as the world geared up for the Second World War her work-load again assumed gigantic proportions. As a Russian diplomat with a partly Finnish background, representing a country the leader of which would probably have liked to see her dead, Alexandra had to steer a tricky route between the demands of the Swedes, those of her Russian masters, and her own conscience.

Thanks to the initial pact between Stalin's Russia and Hitler's Germany, and the Finns' determination to fight the Russians, the situation was both delicate and confusing. Was she supposed to be on the side of the Germans who had, after all, invaded her beloved Norway? Things must have felt easier when the Russians began to fight the Germans. For Kollontai, their military successes were apparently a source of glowing pride.

Kollontai worked tirelessly throughout the Second World War from her base in Sweden, though she was seventy-three when the war ended, and had been in poor health, off and on, for some years. She was prone to palpitations, high blood-pressure, heart-attacks and strokes, but she had a remarkable ability to bounce back, with the help of good doctors and periods of recuperation, for instance in a Swedish spa town.

In the year the second war ended, Kollontai returned to Moscow, to a comfortable small flat on Bolshaya Kaluzhskaya Street which was soon home to her brightly-coloured Mexican paintings. Of course she continued to work, putting her voluminous papers in order, and advising the Soviet foreign ministry, the Commissariat of Foreign affairs. She was also regularly visited by her son Misha, his wife, and their son Volodya, who had built up an impressive stamp-collection thanks to the letters his grandmother had sent home from foreign parts.

It was on International Women's day, the eighth of March 1952, that Alexandra Kollontai, then aged seventy-nine, suffered the massive heart-attack that would end her life early the following morning. She was buried at Moscow's Novodevichii Monastery, where she now sleeps alongside the anarchist Peter Kropotkin, the actor and acting theorist Konstantin Stanislavski, the writer Mikhail Bulgakov, and the composer Sergey Prokofiev, who died on the fifth of March 1953, the same day as Stalin.

Although Cathy Porter's 1980 biography of Kollontai is generally sympathetic, the treatment she receives at the hands of Clive James in his 2012 book *Cultural Amnesia* is extremely hostile. It is of a piece with James's attack on Trotsky in the same book, and is in keeping with a quotation from the French philosopher Jean-François Revel that is printed at the front of the volume: 'One insults the memory of the victims of Nazism if one uses them to bury the memory of the victims of communism'.

Concerned, perhaps, that Kollontai might become an unworthy heroine for modern feminists, James reminds us that she was 'unusually adroit when it came to aligning herself with the prevailing power' and goes on to say that 'her dogged service to a regime that condemned large numbers of innocent women to grim death has rarely resulted in her being criticized by left-wing feminists in the West'.

James does not tell us what else he thought Kollontai could have done once it became obvious that the Russian communist state had become a killing machine. At least he writes about her 'service' rather than her 'support'. Although she was wise enough not to air negative views of Stalin when he was fully established as the murderous communist tsar (and even felt obliged to write and speak in support of Stalinist atrocities, from time to time) Cathy Porter looks closely at the evidence to find clear hints that she did not support him.

Kollontai was not alone in being terrified into writing in favour of Stalin's regime. Ann Akhmatova, born nearly twenty years after Kollontai, also had an ex-husband who was murdered by the Russian authorities, and a son who was liable to be arrested and imprisoned. In fact the poet's son Lev Gumilev was arrested and imprisoned several times.

If they had been genuinely enthusiastic Stalinists, Kollontai and Akhmatova would not have been alone, even in the West. Diego Rivera's wife (and briefly Trotsky's lover) the artist Frida Kahlo died half-way through painting an admiring portrait of the Georgian; the English writer H.G. Wells wrote in support of him, and George Bernard Shaw died in a room that had a photo of the General Secretary on the mantel-piece.

For Kollontai, a highly visible Russian citizen, the alternative to 'dogged service', open criticism of the regime, would probably have seen her subjected to one of the notorious show-trials, then shot, as her husband had been. At the very least, her statements might have meant that she was forced to stop being an ambassador, and made to return to Moscow. There she would have been in far more danger than she ever was in Norway or Sweden. After 1940, she had the example of Trotsky to show her that any attempt to go on the run could end in murder: Stalin's long arm could stretch across wide seas and continents.

And if Kollontai had openly defected, that would have put her son, her daughter-in-law, her grandson and all her friends in Russia in far more danger than they already were. By carrying on doggedly Kollontai was not only escaping danger: she was doing positive good, easing aside some of the heavy folds in what came to be known as the Iron Curtain.

Louise Bryant

The American reporter who befriended Alexandra Kollontai in the midst of the revolution, and found rather more to admire in her than Clive James did (with nearly a century of hindsight) was born Anna Louise Mohan in San Francisco in 1885. She knew comparative poverty and quite a lot of movement from place to place during her childhood, which was also adventurous in some ways. For some years before the age of twelve, she lived with her step-grandfather, James Say, at his mining station near Carson Sink in the Nevada desert. There she rode a horse and chased off coyotes, among other things. Louise's mother, Louisa Flick, had had a similar wild Nevada upbringing.

Bryant's father was a struggling journalist who took to drink and deserted the family when Louise was only four years old. His wife divorced and re-married – this time her husband was a railwayman, Sheridan Bryant, who offered security and even a modicum of prosperity. Bryant was able to attend college in Nevada, and also in Eugene, Oregon, where she struck her contemporaries as glamorous, unconventional and intelligent.

A college photo taken in 1908 shows her with her hair piled up in the gravity-defying style of the time. She is almost the personification of the Gibson Girl of the period – the ideal of beauty invented by the American illustrator Charles Dana Gibson. The difference is that the Gibson Girls didn't have such narrow faces, and they tended to look disdainful – in the 1908 photo, Louise looks as if she is just about to start laughing. Her best feature – her violet eyes – could never be captured by black and white photography. In photos, they often appear so pale that the irises are hard to see at all. A 1913 portrait painted by her first husband's cousin, John Henry Trullinger, shows her posing in an elegant summer outfit against a wall painted a warm violet.

In 1909 Bryant moved to Portland, Oregon, and married a dentist named Paul Trullinger. Despite Paul's very conventional choice of profession, at first the couple lived on a houseboat and mixed with a bohemian set, given to drinking alcohol and indulging in the recreational inhalation of ether (the gas diethyl ether), and uninhibited weekends spent in shacks in the surrounding countryside.

Louise avoided living like a conventional housewife, even when she and her husband moved out of the houseboat and into an actual house. She kept the name Louise Bryant and made money of her own, contributing articles and illustrations to local newspapers. She had her own studio in Portland, and may even have lived apart from Trullinger at times. Bryant also put off having any children and became involved in political causes, including the struggle for votes for women.

Things started to speed up when she met the tall, handsome Jack Reed, a scion of a wealthy local Portland family, and ran off with him to New York in 1915. Reed was a bachelor who was two years younger than his new mistress, though it seems he believed she was two years younger than he was. According to her biographer Mary Dearborn, shaving years off her age was just one of the tricks Bryant indulged in in an attempt to re-create herself in a more exciting form. When he met Bryant, Reed was trying to extricate himself from a relationship with the philandering banking heiress, Mabel Dodge.

It was inevitable that Bryant and Reed would meet at some point. She lived in Portland, and he was a native of the place. They were roughly the same age, both moved in radical circles, and both were journalists, though thanks to his Harvard education, his good connections and the fact that he was a man, Reed was much further along in his career than she was.

Now we should find it in our hearts to feel sorry for the first husbands, wives and partners of remarkable people who get left behind when their ambitious other halves 'outgrow' them. Think of Trotsky's first wife, abandoned in Siberia with their two tiny daughters. Or Ann Shakespeare, stuck in Stratford while her husband trod the boards, penned plays and poems and ran after his Dark Lady down in London. To this sorry list we must add poor Paul Trullinger, the Portland dentist.

Jack Reed

In New York Bryant lived with Reed in Greenwich Village, where the goings-on made bohemian life in Portland, Oregon look like tea at the vicarage. Unmarried couples lived together openly, and some of the radical Villagers believed in free love. The set included some characters whose names may still be familiar, even to European readers, such as the feminist novelist Charlotte Perkins Gilman, the anarchist Emma Goldman, the playwright Eugene O'Neill and the aforementioned heiress Mabel Dodge.

In the spring and summer of 1916, a large portion of the Greenwich Village set decamped to the tiny fishing-village of Provincetown, Massachusetts. There they collaborated in very earnest amateur dramatics, born partly out of a sense of disappointment about the kinds of plays that were then being put on on Broadway in New York. There was a need for new plays, and both Reed and Bryant wrote short pieces that could share an evening's bill with others.

Eugene O'Neill

When it emerged that O'Neill, the son of a leading actor, had a treasure-trove of plays he had written, the so-called Provincetown Players began to put them on, thus starting up O'Neill's illustrious career as a playwright. The playwright and Louise Bryant acted together in a play called *Thirst*, where they played, respectively, a sailor and a dancer stranded on a boat at sea.

Journalism and political activism meant that Reed was frequently away from Provincetown: during one of these absences, Bryant and O'Neill went from sharing the same boat to sharing the same bed. Since they were supposed to believe in free love, Reed could hardly object, and there seem to have been no hard feelings about Bryant's liaison with the intense, hard-drinking O'Neill.

Jack and Louise married in 1916: she had divorced Trullinger earlier the same year. The reasons for the marriage, which they kept secret for a while, were not entirely romantic. Reed had been suffering from kidney problems for years, and the medics had determined that he should have a kidney removed. In those days, survival rates after such operations were low by modern standards, and Reed wanted Bryant to be his wife so that he could name her as his next of kin.

While Jack was away getting treatment at Johns Hopkins in Baltimore, Louise stayed in New York and resumed her relationship with O'Neill, although during this time she too was seriously ill with gynaecological problems. America entered the Great War on April the fourth 1917, and in June Bryant set off alone on the steamer *Espagne*, hoping to be able to cover conditions at the front and solidify her reputation as a serious reporter. The *Espagne* was hunted by a German U-boat on the voyage east, and Louise survived some close shaves, but she never got to the front. She sent articles home to Jack, who edited them and got them published.

By now Reed was well enough to begin philandering again, and at last their infidelities and their endless separations started to take a toll on the relationship. Agonised letters flew across the Atlantic, but when Louise got back in August, in the middle of a ferocious heat-wave, they both seemed to be determined to stick together. Rather than staying put together in New York or elsewhere in the States, or going straight back to the old routine of one waiting at home for the other, they would go together to where the big news story of the moment was happening: revolutionary Russia. Reed gave her the news that they were leaving in four days, just after he greeted his wife on the dock. Young enough to be drafted into the army, Reed was able to avoid conscription because of his missing kidney.

Jack was to report on the situation for *The Masses*, a radical magazine that was in effect closed down by the U.S. government later in 1917, because it was against America's involvement in the war. Thanks to a cash contribution from Eugen Boissevain, a radical coffee magnate of Dutch origin, the magazine was able to fund Reed's trip to the tune of two thousand dollars, equivalent to around forty-five thousand dollars, or thirty-seven thousand British pounds, today. Reed also agreed to send copy to two other journals, but they could not pay him up front. Louise was to write for the then newly-formed Bell Syndicate, which distributed material to a range of publications; and three magazines including the New York *Metropolitan,* for which Reed had written, and which during its history carried material by Joseph Conrad, F. Scott Fitzgerald, Rudyard Kipling, Jack London and Theodore Roosevelt.

Bryant's articles based on her trip to Russia were compiled into a very accessible and relatable book, published in New York in 1918 as *Six Red Months in Russia: An Observer's Account of Russia Before and During the Proletarian Dictatorship* (in fact she spent only four months in Russia). The book gives the impression that Bryant travelled and lodged alone, though it seems that Reed was with her much of the time. With or without Reed, the journey was a risky one. In Russia, there were wars and rumours of wars, and there seemed to be soldiers everywhere, many of whom Bryant remembered as huge, shabby and terrifying. Bryant's reports on Russia took a darker turn in her book *Mirrors of Moscow*, published in 1923, the result of a second visit, during which she revisited a number of important figures, including Trotsky.

When the Americans arrived in the summer of 1917, Russia was looking back on the February revolution that had happened earlier that year, which had led to the abdication of the tsar and the establishment of a Provisional Government, headed by Alexander Kerensky. Various political parties and factions, including the Bolsheviks, were jostling for power amid widespread dissatisfaction with Kerensky and his regime.

An attempt had been made earlier in the summer to wrest power from Kerensky: this took the form of an abortive military coup by Major-General Lavr Kornilov. According to Bryant's account, published in her *Six Red Months in Russia,* Kornilov's troops had deserted him when scouts from Petersburg persuaded them that they should not fight against their brothers, who were loyal to the Provisional Government. A similar version of events appears in Sergei Eisenstein's film *October* (1927) where the hearts of Kornilov's ferocious, battle-hardened men are softened by Bolshevik pamphlets promising peace, land and bread.

Bryant (or rather Bryant and Reed) stayed in a cavernous suite in the Hotel d'Angleterre on St Isaac's Square in the heart of Petersburg. The hotel still exists, though it was rebuilt as a life-size replica of its old self after the fall of the Soviet Union. It has frequently been rebuilt: the writer Leo Tolstoy was a regular guest before it underwent an earlier reconstruction between 1911 and 1912. The husband of one of Tolstoy's granddaughters, the Russian poet Sergei Yesinin, either committed suicide or was murdered in the hotel in 1925.

From the Angleterre, Bryant went out into the streets, noting that there was very little of anything in the shops, and that, now that the workers were in charge, many women paid no attention to their appearance at all, and often looked decidedly shabby and dirty. The makeup of Bryant's female fellow-travellers had been confiscated on entry to Russia, and *maquillage* was seldom seen anywhere in the country.

Food was in very short supply, and the American saw long queues forming for meagre rations. Visiting Russia over sixty years later, I saw similar queues, including one for tiny grey apples covered in brown spots that would never have been offered for sale in the West. Bryant dined on endless coarse, black bread and cabbage soup in workers' canteens, sitting alongside soldiers and workers from every corner of the old tsarist empire.

In Russia in 1980 I noted a strange contrast between the drab food and clothes of the comrades, and the apparent richness of the cultural life of their country. Bryant saw Tamara Karsavina, a Petersburg native, whom she described as 'the most beautiful dancer in the world', performing before 'an audience in rags . . . that had gone without bread to buy the cheap little tickets':

And how she danced and how they followed her! Russians know dancing as the Italians know their operas; every little beautiful trick they appreciate to the utmost. "Bravo! Bravo!" roared ten thousand throats. And when she had finished they could not let her go – again and again and again she had to come back until she was wilted like a tired butterfly.

Readers can get a sense of Karsavina's beauty and power as a dancer by watching videos of her online: some of these pre-date the revolution and many are now over a century old.

It seems that Bryant did not get a chance to interview Karsavina: among the Russian women she did meet was the so-called grandmother of the revolution, Katherine Breshkovsky. Born in 1844, five years before Vera Zasulich, Breshkovsky turned seventy-three in 1917, the year of the October revolution. In 1861 she would have turned seventeen: this was the year of the emancipation of many of the serfs throughout the Russian empire, which took place four years before the abolition of slavery in the United States.

The serfs – a class of people who made up nearly forty percent of the empire's population at the time – had a status close to that of American enslaved people of African descent before 1865. Their lives were not their own – they could be bought and sold together with the estates on which they lived, like livestock or agricultural equipment; and in the nineteenth century it became commonplace for serfs to be bought and sold as individuals.

According to the English-language biography of Katherine Breshkovsky that prefaces a collection of her writings published in 1918, for many ex-serfs the emancipation spelled disaster, and began a period of great insecurity and hardship. Under the old system, they were allotted plots of land to grow their own food. Now many found themselves with much poorer strips of land, and in imminent danger of starvation. The authorities suppressed many of the resulting protests with shocking brutality.

Catherine Breshkovsky

Born into the landed gentry at Vitebsk, over three hundred miles south of Petersburg and west of Moscow, Breshkovsky had always felt compassion for her father's serfs, though she maintained that he treated them comparatively well (Vitebsk is now in Belarus). After two years of marriage to another local landowner, Katherine ran off to Kyiv, now in Ukraine, became involved in radical politics and, during what the anarchist Peter Kropotkin called 'the mad summer of 1874', set off with a group of comrades to 'go to the people' to ferment unrest.

To 'go to the people' Breshkovsky had to leave her tiny son, who had only been born earlier that year, with relatives. At this point, Katherine was a well-educated young lady of thirty, who counted, politically, among the Narodniks, the name of whose movement was inspired by the Russian word for 'people'. The Narodniks themselves were inspired by, among others, the Russian anarchist Michael Bakunin, who was twice Katherine's age when the mad summer of 1874 arrived. Two years earlier, the bear-like anarchist had been expelled from Karl Marx's First International, which his faction had been trying to wrest from the hands of the communists.

To be accepted by the peasants Katherine and her comrades hoped to inspire to rise up and take over the tsarist empire, they had to dress up like peasants and even learn typical craft skills such as country people at the time needed to survive. They also memorised elaborate cover-stories in order to be able to answer such questions as Where are you from? Where are you going? Why are you here?

Under cover in what is now Ukraine, the Narodniks found the going tough even when they were not trying to preach revolution to the peasants. Their accommodation, as offered by more or less hospitable locals, was usually filthy and alive with vermin, and they found much of the food they were given close to inedible. Some of them found trekking long distances on foot with heavy packs extremely wearing, and once they started to preach revolution in cramped, frugal huts they came up against a wall of ignorance, incomprehension and suspicion.

The Narodniks found that, despite the desperate nature of their lives, many peasants were devoted and obedient to the teachings of the Russian Orthodox Church, and that their religious devotion was bound up with a fanatical, unquestioning affection for the tsar, who was then Alexander II, known as 'the liberator', during whose reign the serfs had been converted into free peasants.

Among some peasants, most of whom were still chained down by horrendous poverty and repression, a bizarre story had arisen that stated that Tsar Alexander, their beloved 'little father', had written a set of laws at the time of the emancipation, designed to turn the peasants' world into a kind of earthly paradise. Pages from this book of laws had been torn out by the tsar's wicked officials and the scheming nobles of his court. This was why the country people were still getting the rough end of the stick.

Incredible as it may sound, Breshkovsky and her Narodniks were forever being told about this mythical, redacted book of laws, and when they started to preach revolution to groups of peasants, many were convinced that what they were reading out from their pamphlets was actually the fabled lost pages of the tsar's book of laws.

Later, in 1876, Vera Zasulich's friend Lev Deich and a comrade called Iakov Stefanovich would try to spark a peasant rebellion in the Chigirin area of southern Ukraine by turning up with what they claimed was an official document from the tsar reiterating his supposed good intentions towards the common people, which had been so badly undermined by his officials and fellow-aristocrats.

Deich and Stefanovich's forgery, copies of which were distributed, ordered the peasants, in the name of the tsar, to rise up and claim the rights and lands that he had promised them. But while the 'to the people' movement of which Breshkovsy had been a part met with apathy, suspicion and incomprehension, the scheme of Deich and Stefanovich attracted too many followers, spun out of control and was quickly spotted and suppressed.

Despite her attempts to conceal her true identity, Katherine was betrayed by a simple, instinctive gesture. In Podolia in the west of Ukraine a local policeman seized her by the chin – something a genuine peasant would have accepted as yet another instance of humiliation, that could not be resisted. Katherine flinched away, which aroused the officer's suspicions. When he searched her bags, he found revolutionary literature. Thus began twenty-two long, hard years of exile and imprisonment for the girl from Vitebsk.

In 1885, when she was forty-one, she was visited at the place of her exile in Transbaikal in the far east of Russia by the American explorer George Kennan. Kennan was enormously impressed by Breshkovsky, and wrote in his book *Travels in Siberia* about her courage, fortitude and 'heroic self-sacrifice'. When Katherine was released in 1896, she went straight back to activism, though now she found the peasants 'more intelligent, and more nearly ripe for revolution'. She travelled all over the empire on trains, and had many close shaves when policemen and others tried to arrest her. She became adept at disguise, turning herself into what looked like a bent old woman, in the twinkling of an eye.

As well as transforming herself into an old woman at need, Breshkovsky now turned herself into a Socialist Revolutionary when her own party merged with others to form the Socialist Revolutionary party in 1902. The party was more in tune with the concerns of the peasants than the Social Democrats, who later became the Bolsheviks, because the Bolsheviks were more interested in stirring up a revolution among the proletariat – people like factory workers, from which class Marx and Engels had expected revolutionary changes to emerge. For the tsarist authorities, Bolsheviks, Socialist Revolutionaries and many other parties were seen as a threat, and to avoid arrest Katherine escaped to Switzerland in 1903.

In America she was well-know thanks to the writings of the intrepid George Kennan, and her visit to that country in 1904 was a barnstorming triumph. In Boston, enthusiastic Russian émigrés carried her round and round a hall, and she made friends with, among others, the left-wing feminist Alice Stone Blackwell. It was Alice who brought out a book of reminiscences and letters of her Russian friend, prefaced with a useful biography, as *The Little Grandmother of the Russian Revolution*, in 1917.

Breshkovsky enjoyed an international status comparable to that of later figures such as Gandhi, the South African leader Nelson Mandela, the Dalai Lama or perhaps the exiled Leon Trotsky. Louise Bryant even compared her to Joan of Arc. Both Trotsky and Breshkovsky painted lurid pictures of the horrors of Russian life, and offered hope for the future. Breshkovsky returned to Russia in time for the failed 1905 revolution, and, despite her fame abroad, was arrested in 1908, imprisoned and then exiled once again to Siberia. When the February revolution of 1917 resulted in a Provisional Government, the leader of the new regime, Alexander Kerensky, invited the little grandmother to Petersburg.

When Louise Bryant met her, Katherine was living in a small room in what had been the tsar's Winter Palace; 'the kind of room', Bryant wrote, 'you would pay three dollars a night for in an American hotel'. 'Babushka', as she was called, had turned down much more lavish accommodation in favour of her humble space, where she dined on tea and black bread. Bryant found her welcoming, charming but rather forgetful:

Often she did not remember in the afternoon what she had said in the morning. I once spent a most amusing day in the Winter Palace, accomplishing none of the things I set out to accomplish. I had had an appointment with Babushka at ten o'clock. At ten she was asleep. At eleven-thirty I went in and we began to talk. Five minutes later three French officers came to pay their respects. Babushka said they would stay but a moment. They stayed two hours . . . at three o'clock Babushka appeared and was amazed to see me.

As we shall see, Breshkovsky's absent-mindedness would become a live issue when she testified before the Overman Committee in Washington DC in February 1919. The negative picture of Russia under the Bolsheviks that she presented there and elsewhere meant that she was obliged to round out her life in a final exile – in Czechoslovakia, where she died in 1934, at the age of ninety.

In her *Six Red Months in Russia* Bryant presents a generally benign picture of Katherine Breshkovsky, though she does mention that she smuggled bombs to parts of the tsarist empire. The Socialist Revolutionaries (or SRs) were by no means averse to terrorism, and assassination was one of their preferred tactics. It was after all an SR,

Fanny Kaplan, who shot and nearly killed Lenin in the summer of 1918, and it was four SRs who hanged Father Georgi Gapon in a cottage outside Petersburg in 1906. Secret courts made up of SR members would sit in judgement on certain public figures, condemn them to death in their absence, then send people out with pistols or, in Gapon's case, a willingness to improvise a murder on the spot.

Spiridonova

Maria Spiridonova, whom Louise Bryant came to know well, was a rather more successful SR assassin than Fanny Kaplan. In January 1906, at the age of just twenty-two, she managed to get five bullets into Gavriil Luzhenovsky, a landowner and local official, on the station platform at Borisoglebsk in Voronezh province. Gavriil hung on for less than a month, dying of his wounds on the tenth of February. Maria was so small and slight that she had been able to disguise herself as a schoolgirl in preparation for her fateful encounter with Luzhenovsky.

Although she must have looked like a child, the Cossacks who guarded Luzhenovsky beat her up, stripped her and threw her, naked, into a cell. There they tortured her, trying to extract the names of any accomplices. Among other tortures, they pulled out clumps of her hair and burned her skin with lighted cigarettes. In her account, Bryant says that 'for two nights she was passed around among the Cossacks and the gendarmes', which suggests that she may have been subjected to multiple rapes. There are certainly strong hints that one of her torturers, a Cossack called P.F. Avramov, raped Maria on a train. Probably as a result of all this ill-treatment, Maria, who was frail in any case, became seriously ill.

On the twelfth of February, a Petersburg paper published a letter Maria had been able to smuggle out of prison. This detailed her rough treatment. The word spread and Spiridonova's case caused widespread outrage. It also emerged that her victim, Luzhenovsky, had been notorious for his brutality. As Bryant wrote:

He went from village to village taking an insane, diabolical delight in torturing people. When peasants were unable to pay their taxes or offended him in any way at all, he made them stand in line many hours in the cold and ordered them publicly flogged. He arrested anyone who dared hold a different political view from his own; he invited the Cossacks to commit all sorts of outrages against the peasants, especially against the women.

Spiridonova's letter and Luzhenovsky's notoriety gained a lot of sympathy for the assassin, as more and more papers covered the story. Since she was unmarried, many assumed Maria was a virgin, which allowed her to become a sort of Joan of Arc figure, like Breshkovsky. In fact it is likely that she had previously enjoyed a sexual relationship with a Socialist Revolutionary comrade, Grigory Gershuni, who was married to somebody else.

In Vera Zasulich's case, nearly thirty years earlier, the lurid facts about her victim's behaviour had led her jury to find her not guilty. Maria Spiridonova was not so lucky: she was spared the death penalty, but sentenced to penal servitude in Siberia. According to Bryant, Marie was so ill at the time that she did not even understand that she had been deported. She does, however, seem wide awake in photos of herself with the five other female SR terrorists with whom she proceeded by train to their exile in Transbaikal, three thousand miles east of Petersburg, and much closer to Mongolia and the north-east of China than to anywhere in Europe.

Collectively, Maria and her five fellow-convicts were known as the *Shesterka* or six. The other five were Riva Fialka, Lidiya Ezerskaya, Anastasiya Bitsenko, Manya Shkol'nik and Aleksandra Izmaylovich. In group photographs, Maria looks like she is the smallest – that she is one of the two who wear the *pince-nez* that were fashionable at the time also makes her look older, more authoritative and more intellectual.

Maria Spiridonova spent eleven years in exile in various places. In her *Six Red Months* Bryant implies that, though she often suffered from physical ill-health, including the symptoms of tuberculosis, the main challenge was to keep her mind 'clear'. When Louise asked her how she managed to do this in exile, Maria told her 'I learned languages . . . you see, it is a purely mechanical business and therefore a wonderful soother of nerves. It is like a game and one gets deeply interested. I learned to read and speak English and French in prison'.

Like Katherine Breshkovsky, her senior by forty years, Maria Spiridonova was allowed to return home after the February Revolution of 1917. Bryant met her several times: on the last occasion, they spoke about the progress of the peace negotiations between the Russians and the Germans at Brest-Litovsk, then a German-controlled city, now the city of Brest in Belarus. For Russia, the terms agreed at Brest-Litovsk in March 1918 were utterly humiliating, but at least they got Russia out of the Great War.

Bryant was enormously impressed with Spiridonova, calling her 'the most politically powerful woman in Russia or the world' and admitting that 'I have not met a woman her equal in any country'. Alexandra Kollontai had to take second place after Spiridonova in Bryant's list of admirable women in Russia.

By the time Bryant spoke to her for the last time, the Bolsheviks were in control, but Maria remained a Socialist Revolutionary, trying to make a coalition with the party of Lenin and Trotsky actually work. As the Bolsheviks worked towards a one-party state in Russia, with themselves as the one party, this became more difficult. An attempt by the SRs to rise up against the Bolsheviks in 1918 was a shambolic failure, and from then on Maria and her Socialist Revolutionary comrades lived under a cloud.

Early in 1919, Spiridonova was arrested, tried and imprisoned: she escaped and lived under cover in Moscow for nineteen months, until she was arrested again. Although she came from quite a privileged background – her father had been from the minor Russian nobility – she had been able to pose as a poor peasant woman, until her cover was blown. She was released in November 1921 on the condition that she would stay out of politics, but she was re-arrested in May 1923 and exiled to various places far from both Petersburg and Moscow.

In the darker atmosphere of the thirties, Maria experienced much harsher forms of incarceration under Stalin, and was shot dead in September 1941, together with over one hundred and fifty others. This was known as the Medvedevsky Forest massacre.

As well as well-known Russian women, Bryant made time to talk to extremely humble and obscure ones, during her first trip to Russia. One of the curiosities of the story of the October 1917 revolution was the fact that female soldiers helped to guard the Winter Palace in Petersburg against the Bolshevik revolutionaries. At the time, the palace was home to Kerensky's Provisional Government. The so-called Women's Death Battalion, one of a number of women's battalions formed under Kerensky, was mercilessly mocked in Russian director Sergei Eisenstein's 1928 film *October*, about the 1917 revolution.

In the film, the Bolshevik soldiers who encounter members of the battalion on guard at the palace evidently find the whole idea of them ridiculous, and Eisenstein creates the impression that women in general are too weak and emotional to be part of an army at all. The effect is shockingly old-fashioned. There is even a scene where a female soldier is turned away from her military role by the influence of a romantic statue that inflames her amorous side.

Although its treatment of the women's battalions is offensive to modern eyes, Eisenstein's *October* chimes with at least one of Bryant's impressions of Petersburg. She found the capital's giant statues oppressive, and these play an important role in the film. At times during *October* one gets the impression that Petersburg is a city of the night populated by stationary giants. The film even includes a sequence where a tsarist statue is pulled down, and another where it starts to magically re-assemble itself.

For readers of Russian literature, Eisenstein's use of statues is reminiscent of Pushkin's poem *The Bronze Horseman* and his short play *The Stone Guest*. In the poem, a poor haunted Petersburg clerk believes that a giant equestrian statue of Peter the Great is trying to hunt him down. In the play, based on an episode in Mozart's opera *Don Giovanni*, the famous seducer Don Juan is visited by the statue of a man he has killed in a duel. Statues have recently become very relevant for us in the twenty-first century. As history is being re-examined, numbers of them are being removed or defaced, as we try to discover a new set of historic heroes.

A chapter in Bryant's *Six Red Months* recounts the result of her attempt to track down Russia's women soldiers in Bolshevik-dominated Petersburg. She found some of the remains of Kerensky's battalions, and some new recruits. The new recruits all seemed to wear men's trousers, though the rest of their uniforms were extremely diverse. Some were even wearing ballet shoes. They were waiting for uniforms, especially boots, but there seemed to be little hope of these ever arriving.

Bryant tells us that the female guardians of the Winter Palace surrendered to the Bolshevik revolutionaries before a shot was fired, but she went out of her way to find one battalion member who got into a tussle with a Red Guard soldier and ended up falling out of a window. She found this now disabled young woman, Kira Volakettnova, living with her friend, a Jewish girl called Anna Shub in 'one of the great barnlike unused buildings so common in Petrograd'.

The courtyard of the building was home to a huge pile of snow and rubbish, and one of the downstairs rooms was being used as a chicken-coop. The two friends, who had barely any clothes, were surviving on handouts of bread and firewood from the Red Guards, who felt guilty about what had happened to Kira. Anna told Bryant, 'When you go back to America . . . tell them I am a woman soldier, and I fight only imperialistic invaders.'

Louise returned to America some time before John Reed, to find that her articles on revolutionary Russia had made her a celebrity. Like other visitors to Russia at the time, she had come back with Russian clothes bought dirt-cheap, and she began parading around Greenwich Village in a pair of magnificent embroidered boots and a furry hat. She was photographed in these, looking mischievous and smoking a cigarette.

Bryant's biographer Mary Dearborn asserts that, having in effect lost her father at the age of four, Louise had an exaggerated fear of desertion and isolation. With Reed thousands of miles away, tied down by legal and diplomatic red tape in what would become Oslo, Bryant re-attached herself to Eugene O'Neill, successfully luring him away (for a while) from his then live-in girlfriend, the British-born writer Agnes Boulton, who married O'Neill in April 1918.

People noticed how Boulton resembled Bryant, though she was some years younger than Louise. Certainly both were slim and dark-haired. Perhaps O'Neill was looking for a Louise Bryant substitute? Louise herself also started an on/off affair with the gentle, handsome, married artist Andrew Dasburg, another believer in free love, who had also slept with Mabel Dodge.

When he finally returned to America, Jack quickly resumed his philandering habits, and may even have had an affair with the beautiful red-haired poet Edna St Vincent Millay, then one of the stand-out personalities on the American poetry scene. Dearborn is very indulgent about this behaviour of Reed's, pointing out that he *was* very attractive, and implying that he sometimes went to bed with the women who constantly threw themselves at him out of a kind of misplaced generosity. One is reminded of a comment by a heart-throb of an earlier generation. The poet Byron said, about one Claire Clairemont, 'I never loved her nor pretended to love her—but a man is a man–& if a girl of eighteen comes prancing to you at all hours of the night—there is but one way'.

The success of Bryant's book *Six Red Months in Russia* sent her on the inevitable speaking tour, where she wore herself out addressing packed venues all over the United States. At one point in 1919 she seems to have become one of the later victims of the terrifying Spanish Flu, which killed around fifty million people worldwide during 1918 and 1919.

Rapturously received on her speaking tour, where she sold innumerable copies of her book to audience members, Louise got a frostier reception at a hearing of the Overman Committee, where she testified, like her old friend Katherine Breshkovsky, in February 1919 in Washington DC. This senate sub-committee had been set up by Democrat senator Lee Slater Overman, ostensibly to investigate how German and Bolshevik propaganda might be influencing politics in the United States.

From Bryant's point of view, the committee seemed to be spending a lot of time casting shade on the new Bolshevik regime in Russia. Like a number of others, Louise insisted on testifying in the hope of telling the truth about Russia: too many of the witnesses that were called before her, including her old friend Katherine Breshkovsky, had told horror-stories about life under the soviets.

In a way that was utterly transparent and shameful, the all-male panel of the committee did everything they could to minimise the effect of Bryant's testimony. The transcript reveals that they began by asking Louise about her religious beliefs. This was necessary, explained Senator William H. King of Utah, 'because a person who has no conception of God does not have any idea of the sanctity of an oath, and an oath would be meaningless'.

Louise responded to this outrageous bit of specious mansplaining by remarking 'it seems to me as if I were being tried for witchcraft', and going on to point out that 'I did not hear any other witnesses put through such an ordeal'. When Reed testified, just after Bryant, the senators made a big song and dance about his preference for affirming rather than taking a formal oath. They implied that it was suspicious to do so if, like Reed, one was not a Quaker (Quakers are not supposed to swear oaths).

The senators had obviously been hoping that Bryant would fall into their trap by admitting that she was an atheist, as many socialist were, or were meant to be. She kept out of the trap, but soon she was being questioned about her marital status. In those days, many took a dim view of divorcees, even if they had re-married and were not cohabiting with lovers to whom they were not married. Senator King explained that they were asking about her divorce because 'we want to know something about the character of the person who testifies, so that we can determine what credit to give to the testimony'.

The committee also made sure that they reminded the members of the public who were present that Bryant had very recently been involved in a demonstration in support of votes for women, in Washington itself. During this protest, President Wilson had been burned in effigy.

Bryant's ordeal stretched over two days, February the twentieth and twenty-first. During her questioning, the senators tried every trick in the book to undermine both her and her testimony, once they had tried to discredit her by showing up her attitude to religion and her status as a divorcee. They repeatedly questioned details of her testimony, probing any weak points or inconsistencies.

They wasted time by asking the same questions over and over, especially ones that she had not answered particularly well to start with. There was much further mansplaining, which Bryant called 'lecturing', much of it highly condescending. Louise was told that she was young, and that at least one of the senators pitied her. It was implied that as a woman she could not understand the nature of some US government procedures, and she was assured that the committee was determined to treat her like a lady. She was even asked one question that implied that she was unaware that sometimes people lied.

One question Bryant had to answer before the Overman committee concerned a ridiculous calumny about the Bolsheviks that was then gaining currency in the US. It was believed that the new Russian government intended to 'nationalise' unmarried women over eighteen and force them to engage in free love activities. As Louise pointed out, it was well known that the idea had been borrowed from some anarchists who had nothing to do with the Bolsheviks at all. In discounting the story, she took the opportunity to talk about how far the Russians had come with women's liberation and representation in politics.

The way that this ridiculous story was promoted by reactionary elements in the US is reminiscent of more recent attempts by supporters of US president Donald J Trump to convince voters that Hillary Clinton, his opponent in the 2016 presidential election, was responsible for several murders, that numerous leading Democrats were part of a pagan paedophile ring, and that a deep conspiracy had robbed Trump of victory in the 2020 presidential race by somehow hiding millions of votes.

While Bryant spoke out bravely throughout the hearing, she had to tread more carefully when she was questioned about the testimony of her old friend, Katherine Breshkovsky. 'Babushka' had appeared before the committee just a few days earlier, and had delivered a damning indictment of everything Bolshevik and soviet. According to her, Russia had no schools, no supplies of any kind, and no transport, and was now being run by 'brigands'. The Russian people, she insisted, were desperate for countries like the US to intervene militarily, and restore something like Kerensky's Provisional Government.

By contrast, Bryant believed in non-intervention in Russia. The Bolsheviks were not perfect, but they had emerged from a violent, chaotic time. There was a chance that they could bring peace, stability and renewal. They should be given that chance. The beginning of the soviet government resembled the beginning of the American republic, that had also emerged out of a war.

Such was Breshkovsky's sainted status in America that Bryant only felt able to hint that she was 'deluded' and was being 'used' by the American authorities. Louise knew perfectly well that Katherine had become absent-minded, but there is little evidence of this in the transcript of her testimony before the Overman Committee. Needless to say, Babushka was not questioned about her religious beliefs or her marital status. She was allowed to deliver long uninterrupted speeches, and the numerous large holes in her testimony went unprobed. It would not have been clear to a spectator who had not read up on recent Russian history that as a Socialist Revolutionary, the old lady was almost bound to find fault with the Bolsheviks – she was a member of the opposition.

The Overman Committee was part of the so-called First Red Scare in the United States: it was the grim grandfather of the later, notorious House Un-American Activities Committee under Senator Joe McCarthy. Bryant's feeling that she was being tried for witchcraft was strangely prescient: McCarthy's dire activities became known as 'witch-hunts', and Arthur Miller's 1954 play *The Crucible*, about a genuine witch-hunt in Massachusetts near the end of the seventeenth century, was an attempt to expose the wickedness of what McCarthy was doing. Miller himself had been victimised by HUAC in the nineteen-fifties.

Since the United States had completely sold out to capitalism early in its history as a republic, it was not surprising that some powerful Americans would be panicked by the rise of the Bolsheviks in Russia. Karl Marx had predicted that what he called the 'dictatorship of the proletariat' would arise naturally from some late stage of advanced industrialised capitalism, and theorists like Leon Trotsky believed that it was the responsibility of every socialist state to spread the word about their new way of doing politics. In his 1936 book *The Revolution Betrayed* Trotsky revealed the degree to which in the early days of the revolution, the Russian left had depended on their revolution spreading to Germany at least. The possibility that Russia would inspire a lurch to the left in America persuaded Jack Reed to ally himself with the Socialist Party of America on his return.

The outreach department of the new soviet state was the Communist International or Comintern, founded in 1919. For some, the Comintern meant that Russia had become the capital of the left throughout the world, and Reed and his comrades felt that he should return to Russia and ask the Bolshevik authorities to confirm the validity of their party. This was not the Socialist Party of America, but the Communist Labour Party of America, a splinter-group of which Reed was the best-known member.

By this time the patronising and obstructive treatment Louise Bryant had endured at the hands of the Overman Committee had turned into more overt oppression of individuals and groups that were either left-wing or anarchist. These culminated in the Palmer raids of November 1919 and January 1920, when thousands of people were arrested and hundreds deported, on the authority of US Attorney General A. Mitchell Palmer, who, like Bryant, had testified before the Overman Committee.

Although the US authorities were keen to get large numbers of foreign-born individuals out of the country, they made it impossible for Jack Reed to leave legally. He had to be smuggled back to Russia under an assumed identity, with a forged passport, in October 1919. When it became clear that it might be impossible for Reed to get back to America, where he would almost certainly be tried and locked up, Louise herself got to Russia by subterfuge, posing as the wife of a Swedish businessman.

In keeping with her tendency to embroider her life-story, she later claimed that she had dressed up as a boy and posed as a young sailor, working his passage. Waiting for Reed in Moscow, she researched and made notes that went towards more acclaimed articles for the American press, and her 1923 book *Mirrors of Moscow*.

The pair were re-united in Moscow, now the capital of the new Russian state, in September 1920. She found Reed ragged and emaciated, and eventually his physical condition got much worse. In his book *Ten Days that Shook the World*, he had noted a sign hanging in the Smolny Institute in Petersburg imploring the comrades to keep themselves clean. The fear was that soldiers in particular, travelling to the then capital, would bring with them the vermin and infections that swarmed all over the trenches at the front. On October the seventeenth 1920 Louise Bryant's second husband succumbed to a form of typhus, a disease that thrives in dirty, overcrowded conditions.

His remains were interred in the Kremlin wall in Red Square, after a grand ceremony at which Alexandra Kollontai and others gave speeches. Eight years later, Reed's body would be joined by that of his compatriot Bill Haywood, lion of the Industrial Workers of the World, a US union organisation Reed had always admired. Others who keep Reed company in the Kremlin Wall Necropolis include two more Americans, the Scottish communist Arthur MacManus, Joseph Stalin, and the cosmonauts Yuri Gagarin and Vladimir Komarov.

Louise responded to Jack's death by throwing herself into her work. She was now highly respected as a journalist, able also to turn out worthwhile books like her *Six Red Months*. Working for the Hearst news organisation, she was able to travel all over the world, spending time in Russia and also in the United States. Of course men were attracted by the liberated, glamorous widow, and she was involved with a number of them, including a dashing Moscow-based Turk called Enver Pasha, though it is unclear how far any of these relationships went.

In these years she felt a responsibility to Jack's legacy, and she hunted down and attempted to organise papers he had left behind. She also tried to interest the famous Paramount film company in making a movie based on Reed's book *Ten Days That Shook the World*. At Paramount, that had been founded in 1912 and was then based in New York, she met the brilliant, young, rich executive William Bullitt.

A scion of a monied Philadelphia family, Bullitt was related to both Pocohontas and George Washington, and counted Cole Porter and Charlie Chaplin among his friends. Although he had been under thirty at the time, he had played an important part in negotiations with Russia at the end of the Great War, but the settlement that he had hammered out with Lenin had not been adopted, leaving Bullitt massively disillusioned.

William Bullitt

Bill and Louise were involved for several years before she agreed to marry him. For a time he followed her around the world, as her flourishing journalistic career took her to various places. His wealth and contacts meant that in Istanbul the couple could live amidst the faded glories of an Ottoman palace. They did not marry until 1923, by which time Louise was pregnant with her only child, Anne, born in February 1924. Their marriage meant the formal end to Bryant's career as a journalist. As well as raising Anne, the couple also adopted a handsome little Turkish boy called Refik Ismaili Bey.

Dearborn implies that a part of Bill Bullitt may always have wanted an old-fashioned bourgeois stay-at-home wife; but he was never going to persuade a free spirit like Louise Bryant to turn into one of those. The couple lived for a while as fashionable society people in Paris, holding eclectic soirees in their grand house, but they were soon globe-trotting again. Bullitt was himself too unstable mentally to live in an old-fashioned bourgeois household. Although, according to Dearborn, the family have always denied it, Bullitt sought help with his mental problems and, money being no object, in 1926 he consulted Sigmund Freud himself, whose works had been read so avidly by Alexandra Kollontai.

In Paris in particular, the Bullitts moved in artistic circles, and dabbled to some extent themselves. Louise modelled in clay, and Bill wrote a novel. Bryant also worked hard to promote the career of a Jamaica-born African American author, Claude McKay, noted for writing novels, poetry and short stories. Some of this activity had a dilettante flavour, and for Louise at least it was a far cry from her life after Jack Reed's death. Then she had been a valued and acclaimed journalist, travelling to news hot-spots all over the world, producing work that people were eager to read, work that made a difference. The change was not lost on Bryant, much as she seemed, at times, to be adapting to her new role as rich man's wife. Her sense that marriage to Bullitt had suddenly rendered her life pointless often surfaced in blazing rows with her third husband, and survives in accusatory letters that she sent him.

At around the same time Bullitt sought psychiatric help, when she had turned forty, Louise began to notice some alarming changes to her body. Painful lumps of fat were appearing in odd places; and she was also experiencing mental problems. As usual, the rich couple consulted the very best people, and a physician in London eventually diagnosed Dercum's disease, a very strange, mysterious, devastating and mercifully rare condition, that impacts both the body and the mind.

Even today, it is likely that many cases go undiagnosed, and the cause of Dercum's is still not understood, though it seems to run in families. There is no cure, but the painful lumps of fat, called lipomas, can now be removed using liposuction, a treatment that was not available in Bryant's day. Various drugs have also been tried, many of which did not exist in the twenties and thirties of the last century.

It turned out that Francis Xavier Dercum, the discoverer of the disease, had been born and bred in Bullitt's home town of Philadelphia. When Bill spoke to him on the phone, the good doctor's advice was less than helpful. He suggested that Bullitt 'pray that she die as soon as possible'. Dercum's sufferers are known for abusing drink and drugs, and Louise began to drink heavily. Many of the details of this period are known from the papers Bullitt drew up to support his divorce from Louise. As well as alcohol, she became addicted to the company of the artist Gwen Le Gallienne, a well-known figure in the thriving lesbian scene in Paris.

His wife's affair with Le Gallienne also went into the large dossier about the state of their marriage that Bullitt was secretly preparing, prior to suing Bryant for divorce. This he decided to do in his home town, Philadelphia, where the story of Bryant's disinhibited behaviour was exposed during prolonged testimony. Bryant herself was not contesting the divorce, so there was no legal need for Bullitt to justify himself – he could simply have claimed that his wife had deserted him, and done the whole thing much more discreetly. Instead the impression was created that Louise was an impossible wife and an irresponsible mother, and the upshot was that the divorce became final in March 1930, leaving Bullitt with full custody of their daughter.

Even the briefest summary of Bryant's situation at this time is heartbreaking. She was now twice divorced and once widowed, and her name had been dragged through the mud by her ex-husband. As well as the stigma that attached to divorcees in those days, she had to cope with more stigma related to her drinking and her lesbian relationship. Having once been able to spend a fortune on travel, hotels, new homes and medical and legal help, she now found herself low on funds, living in a

Paris studio with no running water or electricity. She had long ago abandoned her writing career, and now had no legal access to her sole biological child. She also had to cope with the relentless progress of her horrible illness.

Louise's good looks were gradually being wrecked by Dercum's – her situation was therefore similar to that of Lenin's wife, Nadezhda Krupskaya, who had once been very easy on the eyes. There has recently been a trend on internet social media, where participants have pointed out similarities in the looks of well-known modern figures and personalities from history. The current author has weighed in, pointing out the striking likeness of the Danish philosopher Søren Kierkegaard and the actor Macaulay Culkin, star of the *Home Alone* movies.

Social media types have compared Krupskaya as a young woman to the Holywood actor Scarlett Johansson, who has starred in so many films that it is almost pointless to name any. The similarity in appearance between Johansson and Lenin's wife is not entirely surprising – Scarlett has eastern European ancestors on one side. Unfortunately Krupskaya's appearance was radically altered not by the rare Dercum's disease but by thyroid problems, which are a lot more common. Her eyes became very prominent, she gained weight and her face became round and flat-looking. Thyroid problems can also impact a woman's fertility, which may be one reason why Lenin never fathered any children by Krupskaya.

Louise Bryant had bounced back amazingly well after Jack Reed's death, and she showed signs of resilience and self-assertion in the wake of her second divorce. Her apartment, though Spartan, gave her access to like-minded, broad-minded Parisians and ex-pats, she resumed her relationship with Gwen Le Gallienne, and even found the cash to take up flying. One asset she still had at this time was a set of papers relating to Reed, but she was tricked out of these by a conspiracy of Harvard men who were planning a biography of her second husband. Astonishingly, they seemed completely uninterested in anything she might have to say about her time with Reed. The papers at first formed the Louise Bryant papers at Harvard, but they were re-named the John Reed papers, a name they still retain today.

The mental effects of Dercum's disease began to manifest themselves in Louise's case as crippling paranoia. She believed she was being watched by spies, that Le Gallienne was stealing from her and that she was somehow being poisoned. Meanwhile her financial situation was becoming worse, she was evicted from her studio for non-payment of rent, and died of a brain haemorrhage on the afternoon of January the sixth, 1936, at a seedy two-dollar-a-night Paris hotel, the Liberia. She was fifty.

Paramount did not make a film of Jack Reed's book *Ten Days That Shook the World* in the nineteen-twenties, but in 1981 a new generation was introduced to the story of Jack Reed and Louise Bryant in the Paramount movie *Reds*. The film, a lavish three-hour epic, was produced and directed by Warren Beatty, who also had a hand in the script, and starred as Reed himself. That year, Beatty won the Oscar for best director for his work on *Reds*.

As with most Hollywood films of this type, there are plenty of opportunities in *Reds* for the viewer who knows the history to say, 'It didn't really happen like that'. To give two examples: in real life, as we know, Reed told Bryant that he was off to Russia when he greeted her on the dock on her return from covering the Great War. In the film, this happens on a battlefield in Europe; possibly because in those days before CGI it would have been too expensive to recreate a dock with a ship and extras dressed as arriving passengers, all with the right period look. In the film, Diane Keaton as Louise Bryant also makes mincemeat of the Overman Committee, though we know that that is not exactly what happened.

Reds features specially-shot interviews with people who actually knew Bryant and Reed, including Oleg, the son of Alexander Kerensky, the British author Rebecca West, the novelist Henry Miller, and the artist Andrew Dasburg, one of Bryant's lovers. Dasburg was dead at the age of ninety-two before the film came out, which shows that *Reds* could not have been made much later, if fresh footage of interviews with Bryant's contemporaries were ever going to be part of the mix.

The film implies, in places, that Bryant was a mediocre writer until she started to listen to Reed's suggestions for improvement, and that her political ideas were often confused and unfocussed. There are also too many shots of Keaton as Bryant gazing sadly at Beatty as Reed getting caught up in events when, it is suggested, all she wants to do is live quietly with him somewhere.

The suggestion that the film glamourises Reed, Bryant and their relationship is surely beside the point. In their best days, the real Jack Reed and Louise Bryant were glamorous by nature.

Revolutionary Women

To call the three women featured in this book daughters of the Russian revolution is admittedly a little fanciful, since they were all born before the revolution of 1917, and it is not usual for children to be born before their parents. Zasulich. Kollontai and Bryant were all, however, deeply influenced by the revolution, and Zasulich and Kollontai were both part of the radical Russian diaspora before 1917, and had a hand in preparing the ground for that tumultuous event. Both worked with the exiles Vladimir Lenin and Leon Trotsky, and both wrote in support of radical change in their home country.

Although Louise Bryant was not an important part of any movements that contributed to the events of 1917, she was also an important writer, and like her Russian sisters she was not always supportive of the Bolsheviks, who came out on top once the revolutionary dust had settled. Both Zasulich and Kollontai openly opposed important aspects of the Bolshevik approach, though the latter was effectively silenced amid the atmosphere of fear and paranoia that surrounded the rise of Stalin to supreme, unchallengeable power. As things in Russia grew darker, Bryant, in her Overman testimony and elsewhere, asserted her status as a journalist reporting on events. She was never as politically engaged as Jack Reed was.

Though we may question Bryant's commitment to the revolutionary cause, the commitment of both Bryant and Kollontai to the cause of women's liberation is harder to challenge. Kollontai never seems to have lost sight of her idea that a revolution in the home, in the daily lives of women, was necessary to any real revolution in politics and the state. The problem was that though people like Lenin paid lip-service to Kollontai's feminist aspirations, there was in fact a lot of resistance to the idea of the liberated woman both from Russian revolutionaries of various types and from adherents to the old tsarist way of doing things. The battle-ground where these conflicts were really acted out will be depressingly familiar ground to many people today who resent the way that women's personal options continue to be restricted.

In many contexts, women with important, demanding full-time jobs continue to have to do the lion's share of housework, child-rearing and food preparation. One way women can suddenly find themselves tied down to house and home is by giving birth to a baby. Although they all slept with men, our three daughters of the revolution produced only two children between them. The one who remained childless was Vera Zasulich. Surely this would have helped them all to avoid an excessive amount of nappy-washing domesticity.

As well as avoiding giving birth to babies (in Zasulich's case avoiding it altogether) our three daughters of the revolution also eschewed conventional long-term monogamous marriage, or sticking with just one romantic partner for most of their lives. True, Louise Bryant may have stuck with Jack Reed if he had not died, but their relationship was hardly monogamous. Vera Zasulich never married at all, and both Kollontai and Bryant were divorced twice. The pattern of divorce, one child and a succession of lovers was also followed by the poet Anna Akhmatova.

The low birth-rate possible for Akhmatova, Kollontai, Zasulich and Bryant was down to the range of birth-control methods available to women, in those days before the introduction of oral contraceptives. Contraception, it seems, did not start with the pill. Havelock Ellis, the English sex expert whose works were well-know to Alexandra Kollontai, noticed the widespread take-up of these methods, in Britain at least, during the 1870s. Of course if either Kollontai or Bryant had produced more children, they may have been able to employ servants to look after them for much of the time. A major focus of Kollontai's work was her fight to secure such freedom from the kid-bound condition for ordinary women workers.

Part of the solution as as she saw it was well-run workplace crèches and communal living for families, who were to be discouraged from living as a nuclear family unit. In this way, as in the commune envisaged by eponymous heroine of Kollontai's novel *Vasilisa Malygina,* child-rearing would be everyone's responsibility, and there would always be willing 'uncles' and 'aunties' on hand to change nappies and help with homework. Although communes do exist in the West today, and informal friendship and extended family groups can help hard-pressed parents, well-run workplace crèches still seem to be beyond the capability of many employers, and families shell out huge fees to child-minders and nurseries, even in places like the UK where school-age education is provided free of charge.

Even in the West, where we are supposed to be more enlightened about these things, working women in work-places with or without crèches continue to be paid less for the same work, and are passed over for the top jobs. As we have seen, Alexandra Kollontai was the only woman in Lenin's first cabinet. In the current UK cabinet (in December 2023) only ten of the thirty-two members are women, and the top jobs – prime minister, deputy PM, chancellor of the exchequer and foreign and home secretary, are all occupied by men. At least US president Biden's current cabinet is equally balanced, as is the shadow cabinet of UK Labour Party leader Kier Starmer. In the current Labour shadow cabinet, Starmer's deputy, and the shadow chancellor and home secretary are all women.

Outside of the West, the situation of women in many countries is still a cause for grave concern. 2023's Nobel Peace Prize has been awarded to the Iranian woman Narges Mohammadi, who has campaigned for years against the oppression of women in her own country, symbolised for many by the fact that it is still compulsory for women in Iran to cover their hair with hijab scarves. As I write, Narges is still in prison in Iran. The condition of Muslim women from the old tsarist empire who woke up to find themselves being governed by the Bolsheviks was a major concern for Alexandra Kollontai.

Whereas Kollontai was in a position to argue for new, progressive legislation, Louise Bryant had less influence but, as we have seen, still campaigned for women's rights in her own country. When she was concentrating on her journalism she was still promoting the feminist cause, because in Russia and other places from which she reported she was shedding light on the contribution and predicament of local women. Even if, in Russia, she had only written about the top men, the fact that she was an effective female reporter was still an argument for feminism. Confronted by illness, widowhood, scandal, rejection and poverty, Bryant showed weakness and bitterness in ways Kollontai never really did, but she continued to fight to be independent. Perhaps the greatest challenge for Bryant was, paradoxically, the lure of life as a rich man's spouse. Only when she was in that role did she waste time playing the part of shallow socialite, embracing high fashion and dilettantism.

The charge that will be routinely levelled against either men or women who were involved in the Russian revolution of 1917 and its aftermath is that they were guilty of supporting a regime which grew progressively dictatorial and murderous. Much of this can be laid at the door of Stalin, but by no means all. As we have seen, both Lenin and Trotsky reinforced their power with buttresses made out of dead bodies. It is hard to refute the charge, but it is as well to remember what Bryant said in front of the Overman Committee in 1919. The revolution had been born out of war, and in war there are few decisions the results of which will not involve killing. Bryant reminded the U.S. senators that their own brave republic had born out of just such a violent period. Vera Zasulich was not guilty of supporting Bolshevism in peace-time, as she died in 1919 and she had openly split with the party before her death.

As the dust of war settled and Russia's external threats receded, many found that support for the communists was no longer sustainable. For many in Russia itself, the merest suspicion of such back-pedalling meant arrest and an early death. While Zasulich died before the Stalinist terror, Bryant left Russia just after a key event which is often forgotten, but which comprised an important step towards the one-party Bolshevik state.

As we have seen, the Constituent Assembly, an attempt at a democratically-elected parliament for Russia, was suppressed by the Bolsheviks after it had been established for just a few hours in the winter of 1917-18. Dominated by Socialist Revolutionary members, with a minority of Bolsheviks, it was evidently an embarrassment to Lenin and the Bolshevik leadership. But it was in the period when the Constituent Assembly was still awaited, and a western-style multi-party democracy still seemed possible in Russia, that figures like Zasulich, Kollontai and Bryant were most relevant, and their lives and actions most justifiable.

Select Bibliography

Bakunin, Mikhail: *Statism and Anarchy*, Cambridge, 1990

Bryant, Louise: *Mirrors of Moscow*, Thomas Seltzer, 1923

Bryant, Louise: *Six Red Months in Russia*, Benight, 2019

James, Clive: *Cultural Amnesia*, Picador, 2008

Kollontai, Alexandra: *The Autobiography of a Sexually Emancipated Communist Woman*, Translated by Salvator Attansio, Herder and Herder, 1971

Kollontai, Alexandra: *A Great Love*, Virago, 1981

Kollontai, Alexandra: *Red Love*, Seven Arts, 1927

Lenin, V.I.: *What Is to be Done?*, Martin Lawrence, 1930

Lih, Lars T.: *Lenin* (Critical Lives), Reaktion, 2011

McNeal, Robert H.: *Bride of the Revolution*, Gollancz, 1973

Porter, Cathy: *Alexandra Kollontai: A Biography*, Virago, 1980

Siljak, Ana: *Angel of Vengeance*, St Martin's Press, 2008

Stephenson, Graham: *History of Russia, 1812-1945*, Macmillan, 1969

Stone Blackwell, Alice (ed.): *The Little Grandmother of the Russian Revolution: Reminiscences and Letters of Catherine Breshkovsky*, T. Fisher Unwin, 1918

Trotsky, Leon: *My Life*, Thornton Butterworth, 1930

Turgenev, Ivan: *Fathers and Sons*, translated by C.J. Hogarth, Dent, 1921

Webb, Simon: *Karl Marx in London*, Langley Press, 2023

Wheen, Francis: *Karl Marx*, Fourth Estate, 2000

For more from the Langley Press, please visit our website at
www.langleypress.co.uk

www.ingramcontent.com/pod-product-compliance
Lightning Source LLC
Chambersburg PA
CBHW032021090426
42741CB00006B/692

*9 7 8 1 8 3 8 3 8 5 7 9 8 *